DK

TOP 10
ISTANBUL

W0113958

CONTENTS

Introducing Istanbul

Top 10 Highlights

44

Top 10 of Everything

64

Area by Area

106

Streetsmart

ISTANBUL

INTRODUCING

Galata Bridge and the Golden Horn

WELCOME TO
ISTANBUL

Straddling the border between Europe and Asia, Istanbul is where everything collides: continents; Christianity and Islam; the cultural arts of East and West. Don't want to miss a thing? With Top 10 Istanbul, you'll enjoy the very best the city has to offer.

"If one had but a single glance to give the world, one should gaze on Istanbul", said 19th-century French statesman and poet, Alphonse de Lamartine. Few cities have ruled over one far-reaching empire, but Istanbul has reigned over two, and its time as the capital of both the Byzantine and Ottoman empires has blessed the city with a beauty and diversity quite like anywhere else on the continent. A short walk through the historic district of Sultanahmet will take you from the Ayasofya (Haghia Sophia), one of the most striking mosques in the world,

Shopping in Istanbul's historic Grand Bazaar

to the Topkapı Palace, a sumptuous sultan's residence. Elsewhere, the medieval Galata Tower lies mere blocks from the Istanbul Modern Art Museum.

Above all, though, Istanbul is a melting-pot metropolis, where you can still find vine-tangled caravanserai tucked down alleyways, and shop for saffron and rose buds in one of the oldest covered markets in the world. Here, ancient mysticism – in the forms of Sufi whirling dervishes – blends with hipster coffee shops and the art galleries of Karaköy. This is a place where old and new, tradition and innovation, coexist. A place where Muslims, Christians and Jews live shoulder to shoulder, where skyscrapers share the skyline with ancient domes, minarets and Ottoman palaces, and family-run cafés are just as cool as sleek rooftop bars. The soundtrack here is the call to prayer echoing from mosques, and the squawks of seagulls pirouetting over ferries crossing the blue Bosphorus Strait.

So, where to start? With Top 10 Istanbul, of course. This pocket-sized guide gets to the heart of the city with simple lists of 10, expert local knowledge, and comprehensive maps, helping you turn an ordinary trip into an extraordinary one.

THE STORY OF
ISTANBUL

Set at the crossroads of Europe and Asia, Istanbul has been the capital of two mighty empires. Shaped by the Byzantines, the Romans and the Ottomans, this dynamic destination has grown into the largest city in Europe. Here's the story of how it came to be.

Early History

Artifacts dating back some 8,000 years have been found on the shorelines of modern-day Istanbul, but the oldest settlement here dates from roughly 5500 BCE. In around 1000 BCE, the Thracians, an early people from southeastern Europe, settled a town called Lygos, near Topkapı Palace on the European side. Byzas the Greek, King of Megara, arrived in 660 BCE, built an acropolis on the Thracian ruins and called it Byzantium, thus marking the start of the city's recorded history. In 70 BCE, it became part of the Roman Republic (precursor to the Roman Empire) but remained a free city until 193 CE, when the politician Septimius Severus staged a coup and a two-year civil war ensued. The leaders of Byzantium backed the wrong man,

and the town was besieged and left in ruins. Five years later, Septimius rebuilt it and named it Augusta Antonina, in tribute to his son.

Rise of the Byzantines

The power struggle that followed the abdication of the Roman Emperor Diocletian in 305 was won by Constantine the Great. He united the eastern and western empires (split in two by Diocletian) and selected Byzantium as the new capital in 324, calling it "Nova Roma" (New Rome). In 330, it was renamed Constantinople in his honour – remarkably, the name endured until 1930. To revive the now-walled city, Constantine gifted land to noblemen, offered free food rations to residents and transferred art and statues here from Rome, including the

The Obelisk of Theodosius and the Hippodrome

The Ottoman Army captures the city during the Fall of Constantinople

Obelisk of Theodosius, which is all that survives of the great Hippodrome that now lies beneath Sultanahmet Square. Constantinople became the largest and wealthiest city in Europe, with a population of 500,000 that was governed by Roman law, was largely Christian and spoke Greek. Justinian I completed the Greek Orthodox church Haghia Sophia in 537, which remained the world's largest cathedral for a thousand years.

Decline of the Byzantines

By 1025, the city had started to decline, and in 1204 the Fourth Crusade's attempt to recapture Jerusalem went awry and the unpaid Crusaders sacked Constantinople, converting Haghia Sophia to a Roman Catholic church. Meanwhile, the Genoese (from modern-day Liguria in Italy), who had charmed previous Byzantine emperors into granting them a colony around Galata in 1155, exploited their participation in the Crusade to regain power. They built the Galata Tower in 1348 and became lively participants in Silk Road trading.

In 1299, Osman I founded the Ottoman Empire in Anatolia, and by the 14th century, the Ottoman Turks had begun strangling Constantinople's supply routes. The Ottoman Army, led by 21-year-old Sultan Mehmet II, captured the city in 1453 after a siege known as the Fall of Constantinople.

1000 BCE
Thracians settle the town of Lygos on a site near the modern-day Topkapı Palace.

660 BCE
Byzas, the Greek King of Megara, founds Byzantium.

324 CE
Constantine the Great chooses Byzantium as the capital of his unified Roman Empire, which is later renamed Constantinople.

537
After the Nika Riots, Justinian I finishes building the Greek Orthodox Haghia Sophia.

1453
Following the Fall of Constantinople, the city becomes part of the Ottoman Empire, under the reign of Sultan Mehmet II.

1913
A coup d'état by the ultra-nationalist Committee of Union and Progress (CUP) installs The Three Pashas into power.

1928
Constantinople is renamed Istanbul, five years after Mustafa Kemal Atatürk moves the Turkish capital to Ankara.

1973
Today's July 15 Martyrs' Bridge is built across the Bosphorus Strait, uniting Istanbul's Asian and European sides for the first time.

2010
Istanbul is selected as a European Capital of Culture and hosts an array of events throughout the year.

2024
After more than 20 years in power, President Erdoğan, of the Justice and Development Party, loses control of Istanbul in local elections.

Ottoman Empire

Within hours of capturing Constantinople, Sultan Mehmet II had Haghia Sophia converted into a mosque (Ayasofya). He repopulated the almost-deserted city by relocating Muslim, Jewish and (Greek) Christian citizens from conquered territories, and reconstructed the Grand Bazaar. Significantly, the sultans boycotted trade with China and ended their participation in the Silk Road. Under the rule of Süleyman the Magnificent (1520–1566), many mosques were constructed, and arts, such as calligraphy and ceramics, flourished.

Connecting to Europe

By the 19th century, reforms and modernizations – such as the long-overdue supply of electricity – were underway, while the construction of the Golden Horn bridge and a railway connected Constantinople to Europe. These advancements, however, were not enough to quell college students and dissident soldiers who were growing frustrated with an old-fashioned constitution and the 30-year closure of parliament following the Russo-Turkish War.

Sultan Mehmet II entering Constantinople

Istanbul's skyline, a mix of ancient and contemporary

In 1908, the Young Turk Revolution withdrew powers from the sultanate, forcing him to restore the 1876 constitution and finally recall parliament. Following a 1913 coup d'état, the country was led for a while by a trio of Young Turk ministers, nicknamed The Three Pashas. They led Turkey into World War I, on the side of Germany, and instigated a policy of Turkification that resulted in the exodus of Christians from the city and the genocide of more than a million Armenians across the Ottoman Empire.

Founding of the Turkish Republic

Following the end of World War I, Constantinople was occupied by Allied forces until the signing of the Treaty of Lausanne in October 1923. The Turkish War of Independence (1919–1922) and the exiling of Mehmet VI, the last sultan, to Italy effectively marked the end of the Ottoman Empire. On 29 October 1923, Mustafa Kemal Atatürk, a field marshal in the Turkish army, founded the Republic of Turkey and moved the capital to Ankara; Constantinople was renamed Istanbul in 1928. After Turkey took a neutral role in World War II, the 1950s saw an expansion of Istanbul, with the development of new public squares such as Taksim. However, this optimism was marred by the 1955 pogrom, a genocide of Greek residents in retaliation for the bombing of a Turkish consulate in Greece. Trade increased with the construction of the first Bosphorus bridge in 1973, and in 1985 Istanbul's historical centre was named a UNESCO World Heritage Site.

Istanbul Today

With a population of 15.6 million, Istanbul is currently the largest city in Europe. It continues to tackle the challenges of adapting an ancient city to accommodate modern life, and its position between Europe and Asia can make it something of a tinder box, with the city suffering a handful of terrorist attacks in recent years. Much has been shaped by President Erdoğan, who has been in power for more than two decades. Increasingly authoritarian, he has been criticized for his strict control of the media and for mismanaging the worst economic crisis in the nation's history. He has also been plagued by accusations of corruption. However, change is afoot. Erdoğan lost control of Istanbul in the 2024 local elections and his term as president is scheduled to end in 2028.

TOP 10
EXPERIENCES

Planning the perfect trip to Istanbul? Whether you're visiting for the first time or making a return trip, there are some things you simply shouldn't miss out on. To make the most of your time – and to enjoy the very best this exciting city has to offer – be sure to add these experiences to your list.

1 Soak up the hammam culture

Introduced by the Persians in the 15th century, hammams were the city folk's primary source of sanitation – a place to be steamed, soaked and scrubbed – but they also served as halls of story-telling and music. Try it for yourself at historic Çemberlitaş (p38).

2 Ride a ferry between two continents

Commuting Istanbulites use the ferries that zip across the Bosphorus (p42) daily, but they're also an ideal (and cheap) way to explore the fringes of the city – and to say that you've straddled the border between Europe and Asia.

3 Taste the world's best baklava

Baklava – honey-soaked, layered filo pastry, filled with pistachios, walnuts or hazelnuts – is a must-try Ottoman sweet treat. US chef Anthony Bourdain deemed the city's best to be found at Karaköy Güllüoğlu (p97), a family-run cafe in operation since 1843.

4 Enjoy an underground concert

The Basilica Cistern (p69), built during the Byzantine era, served the Great Palace of Constantinople. It's a hidden world, where a soaring vaulted ceiling and many columns provide unique acoustics, which are shown off at regular concerts.

5 See a whirling dervish

Entranced in a form of dynamic meditation designed to bring them closer to God, the whirling dervishes *(p58)* date back to the 13th century. In full-circle white skirts and tall felt hats, they spin at dizzying speeds. Sitting in on a session is utterly hypnotic.

6 Take a food tour

Istanbul's history and cultural identity is evident in its food *(p56)*. Learn about both with a tastebud-tingling tour with Culinary Backstreets *(culinarybackstreets.com)*, where you'll be treated to a smorgasbord of small plates and interesting anecdotes.

7 Explore Kadıköy

Ditch the crowds and catch the ferry to Kadıköy *(p102)*. Istanbul's hippest neighbourhood spreads along the Asian side of the Bosphorus and is home to the city's cool crowd, who have lined its modern streets with street art, hipster cafés and bars.

8 Breakfast like a local

Breakfast, or *kahvalti*, is a feast of cheeses and cured meats, olives, honey, pastries and eggs, all washed down with endless flutes of black tea. Try Hasan Fehmi Özsüt *(p93)*, open since 1915 and run by the same family for three generations.

9 Ride the world's second-oldest subway

Don't want to climb the hill to Beyoğlu? No problem. The Tünel *(p90)* between Karaköy and Beyoğlu is the oldest underground train in continental Europe and the second-oldest in the world after the London Underground.

10 Sip sundowners on a rooftop bar

Istanbul's crenellated skyline of minarets mixed with high-rises was built to be seen from above. Head up to a rooftop bar *(p59)*, best at golden hour, when the honeyed sun sets the mosque domes aglow.

ITINERARIES

Visiting the Blue Mosque, browsing the Grand Bazaar, cruising on the Bosphorus: there's a lot to see and do in Istanbul. With places to eat, drink or simply take in the view, these itineraries offer ways to spend 2 days and 4 days in the city.

2 DAYS

Day 1

Morning
Start the day with tales of intrigue at the ultra-opulent Topkapı Palace *(p22)*, once home to Ottoman sultans and their concubines. It's just a few steps from here to the Ayasofya (Haghia Sophia), a 1,500-year-old museum-turned-mosque *(p26)*; non-Muslims are only granted access to the upper gallery and its Byzantine mosaics, but this is still a must-see sight for everyone. Cross the road and descend below street level to explore the eerie Basilica Cistern *(p69)* – just don't let its Medusa heads turn you to stone.

Afternoon
After a casserole lunch at nearby Palatium *(p73)*, cover up to enter the iconic Sultan Ahmet Mosque, better known as the Blue Mosque *(p28)*, to

> **EAT**
> Snack on *balık ekmek* (grilled mackerel sandwiches) on Galata Bridge, roasted chestnuts from street vendors on İstiklal Caddesi in winter or *dondurma* (Turkish ice cream) across the city in summer.

gaze at its thousands of blue İznik tiles. Unwind after your day of sightseeing at nearby 16th-century Çemberlitaş *(p38)*, a hammam where attendants will soap you up then rub you down. Sudsed and soothed, finish the day with a roasted *cağ* kebab at the no-frills-but-lauded Şehzade Cağ Kebap *(p85)*.

Day 2

Morning
Dive right into the labyrinthine Grand Bazaar *(p32)*, where people have been trading goods since the 15th century, and practise the art of haggling with some of the thousands of stall owners. Then cross the Galata Bridge *(p76)*, a 15-minute walk north of the bazaar, and shell out a lira to ride the Tünel tram *(p90)*, the world's second-oldest underground, between Karaköy and Beyoğlu. From the top, it's a short walk to the medieval Galata Tower *(p87)*. Flash your Istanbul Tourist Pass *(p61)* for free entry and take the elevator to the 7th floor – save your legs for the last two levels and the sublime skyline views from the top.

Baklava on sale at a stall in the Grand Bazaar

Shoppers passing Ciçek Pasaji, on İstiklal Caddesi

Afternoon

Back on ground level, stop for lunch at Kafe Ara *(p93)* on your way up İstiklal Caddesi for a browse inside Ciçek Pasaji *(p90)*, a glamorous 19th-century shopping arcade. Further north lies Taksim Square *(p89)*, site of political clashes that have helped shape modern Istanbul. You can cross the square to Atatürk Cultural Centre *(p92)* for a refined dinner with city views from its rooftop restaurant, Biz, or hop on the tram back to Eminönü Station and nearby Pandeli *(p79)*, which serves Michelin-listed Turkish classics, such as slow-cooked lamb and aubergine pie, above the entrance to the Spice Bazaar.

> **VIEW**
> The Galata Bridge, often bristling with rows of anglers, offers 360-degree views of Istanbul: back to Sultanahmet; across to Beyoğlu; up the Golden Horn and out over the Bosphorus.

Taksim Square
Biz
Atatürk Cultural Centre
İstiklal Caddesi
Taksim
FUNICULAR
Kabataş
Kafe Ara
Ciçek Pasaji
BEYOĞLU
TRAM
Beyoğlu
Galata Tower
FUNICULAR
Tünel Tram
Karaköy
KARAKÖY
Golden Horn
Bosphorus
Galata Bridge
Eminönü
Pandeli
EMİNÖNÜ
Spice Bazaar
Şehzade Cağ Kebap
BEYAZIT
Topkapı Palace
1
Grand Bazaar
2
Basilica Cistern
Çemberlitaş Hammam
Ayasofya (Haghia Sophia)
ÇARŞIKAPI
Palatium
Blue Mosque
SULTANAHMET

0 metres   700
0 yards   700

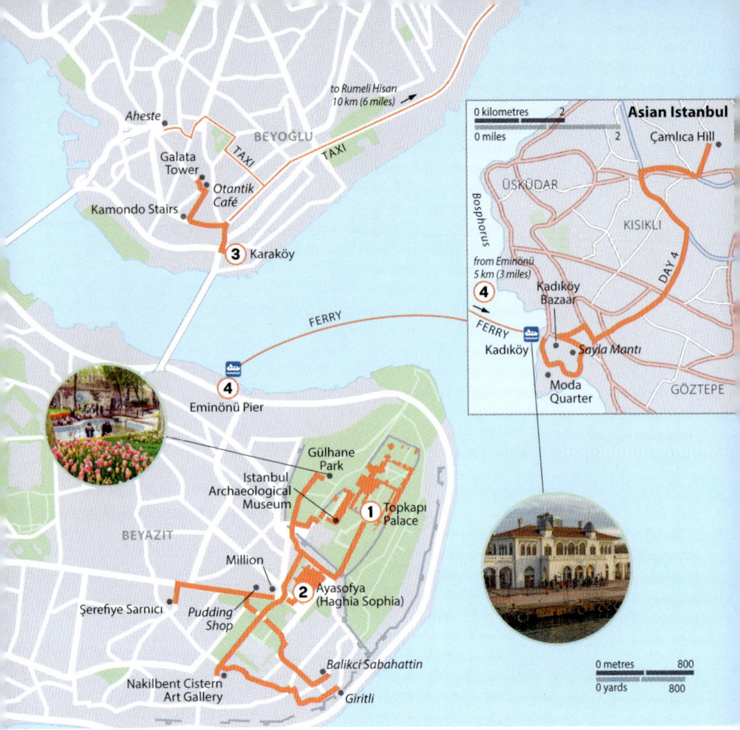
to Rumeli Hisarı 10 km (6 miles)
Aheste
BEYOĞLU
TAXI
TAXI
Galata Tower
Otantik Café
Kamondo Stairs
3 Karaköy
FERRY
4 Eminönü Pier
Gülhane Park
Istanbul Archaeological Museum
1 Topkapı Palace
BEYAZIT
Million
2 Ayasofya (Haghia Sophia)
Şerefiye Sarnıcı
Pudding Shop
Balikci Sabahattin
Nakilbent Cistern Art Gallery
Giritli
0 metres 800
0 yards 800
0 kilometres 2
0 miles 2
Asian Istanbul
Çamlıca Hill
ÜSKÜDAR
Bosphorus
KISIKLI
from Eminönü 5 km (3 miles)
4
DAY 4
Kadıköy Bazaar
FERRY
Kadıköy
Sayla Mantı
Moda Quarter
GÖZTEPE

4 DAYS

Day 1

Kick things off with a peek into sultan life at the Topkapı Palace *(p22)*, one of the world's largest surviving royal residences, and ask an attendant about its precious Piri Reis map, a 16th-century world map drawn on gazelle skin that was found when the palace was converted into a museum in 1929. Refuel at one of the tea-garden cafés at the northern end of neighbouring Gülhane Park *(p70)*, famed for its nesting storks and white roses, before popping into the Istanbul Archaeological Museum *(p30)* to see the mammoth marble Alexander Sarcophagus. From here, it's a 20-minute walk, beyond the Blue Mosque, to the 6th-century Nakilbent Cistern Art Gallery *(Nakilbent Sok 6)*, which is tucked away in the basement of the Nakkaş carpet shop. End the day with a *meze* spread at Giritli *(p73)*, a Cretan restaurant inside a restored Sultanahmet house.

EAT

Try the city's best *simit* (a twisted bread ring coated in sesame seeds) at friendly Galata Simitçisi on Mumhane Caddesi.

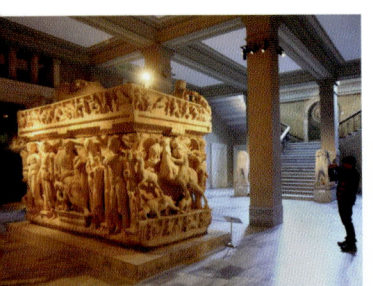

Alexander Sarcophagus, Istanbul Archaeological Museum

Day 2

Beat the crowds and visit the Ayasofya (Haghia Sophia) as soon as it opens its doors after prayers *(p26)*. Outside, just across the tram tracks that run all the way along Divanyolu Caddesi, seek out the oft-overlooked Milion *(p70)*, all that remains of a 4th-century monument that marked the starting point for all roads leading to Byzantine towns. Just around the corner from here is the famous Lale Restaurant *(p72)*, better known as the Pudding Shop, a hippy-trail hangout where travellers would hitch rides across Turkey and Asia; today, it's a fun albeit-touristy spot for lunch. In the afternoon, walk west to the 1,600-year-old Şerefiye Sarnıcı *(serefiyesarnici.istanbul)*, a ghostly cistern with soaring Corinthian columns and an arty 10-minute 3D projection show. Wander back towards the Bosphorus to crown off the day with superlative seafood small plates at the unfussy but award-winning Balıkçı Sabahattin *(p73)*.

Day 3

Start the day in atmospheric Karaköy *(p97)*, one of Istanbul's oldest districts. Take the time to explore its nooks and crannies and you'll uncover street art and hidden Silk Road *caravanserai* that house art studios and boutique shops – plus the city's best baklava. Head up the hill to Bankalar Caddesi and climb the Gaudi-esque Kamondo Stairs *(p97)* towards the Galata Tower *(p87)*. After taking in the epic city views from the top of the tower, and a bite to eat at nearby Otantik Café *(p93)*, hail a taxi

to Rumeli Hisarı *(p96)*, a 15th-century Ottoman fortress built in the shape of the name of Prophet Mohammed, which delivers sweeping views from its crenellated walls. Return to Karaköy, via taxi again, for dinner at romantic Aheste *(p93)* – book ahead, and treat yourself to the gourmet *meze* tasting menu featuring dishes such as Persian rice and tuna *kadayıf*.

Day 4

Take it easy on your final day in Istanbul and set sail between two continents on a Bosphorus cruise *(p42)*, departing from Eminönü Pier. Disembark in up-and-coming Kadıköy *(p102)*, on the Asian side, and browse the galleries and boutiques of the Moda quarter. Wander among the stalls of Kadıköy Bazaar, but save some energy for the climb up Çamlıca Hill, a vantage point that offers stellar views of the city's European side. Bring your trip to a tasty end at low-key Sayla Mantı *(saylamanti.com.tr)* with a dinner of traditional *manti*, mini dumplings topped with garlicky yoghurt and melted butter.

A Bosphorus cruise, passing the Galata Tower and Galata Bridge

TOP 10 HIGHLIGHTS

Interior of the Ayasofya (Haghia Sophia)

EXPLORE THE
HIGHLIGHTS

There are some sights in Istanbul you simply shouldn't miss, and it's these attractions that make the Top 10. Discover what makes each one a must-see on the following pages.

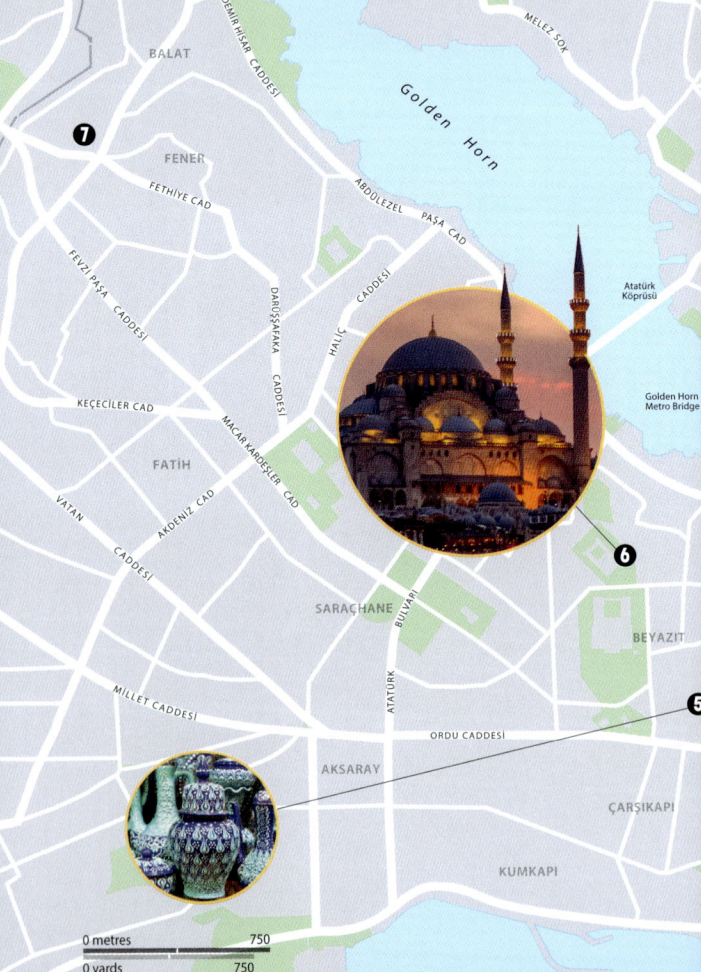

Golden Horn

MELEZ SOK

BALAT

DEMİR HİSAR CADDESİ

FENER

FETHİYE CAD

ABDÜLEZEL PAŞA CAD

Atatürk Köprüsü

Golden Horn Metro Bridge

FEVZİ PAŞA CADDESİ

DARÜŞŞAFAKA CADDESİ

HALİÇ CADDESİ

KEÇECİLER CAD

MACAR KARDEŞLER CAD

FATİH

AKDENİZ CAD

VATAN CADDESİ

SARAÇHANE BULVARI

BEYAZIT

ATATÜRK BULVARI

MİLLET CADDESİ

ORDU CADDESİ

AKSARAY

ÇARŞIKAPI

KUMKAPI

0 metres   750
0 yards   750

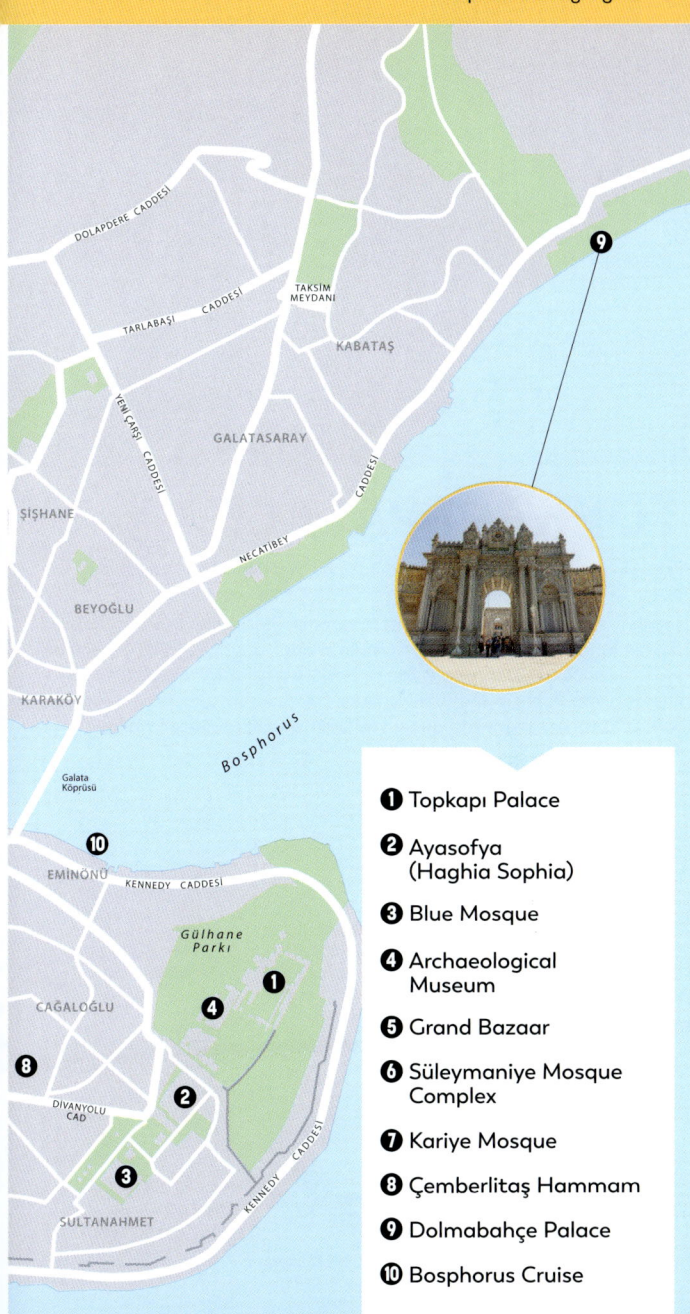

1 Topkapı Palace

2 Ayasofya (Haghia Sophia)

3 Blue Mosque

4 Archaeological Museum

5 Grand Bazaar

6 Süleymaniye Mosque Complex

7 Kariye Mosque

8 Çemberlitaş Hammam

9 Dolmabahçe Palace

10 Bosphorus Cruise

TOPKAPI PALACE

🅿 S3 🏠 Babıhümayun Cad 🕐 9am–5:30pm Wed–Mon 🌐 millisaraylar.gov.tr 🔗🔗🔗

Fresh from his conquest of Constantinople, Mehmet II built Topkapı Sarayı in 1460 and used it as his main residence until 1478. This palace was the seat of government for 400 years until that role passed to the Sublime Porte in the 16th century. Topkapı remained the sultan's palace until Abdül Mecit I moved to Dolmabahçe Palace in 1856.

1 Imperial Gate (Bâb-ı Hümayun)

Built in 1478, this imposing gate is the main entrance to the palace. An apartment belonging to Mehmet II above the gate was destroyed by fire in 1866.

3 Gate of Salutation (Bâb-üs Selâm)

At this ornate gate, built in 1524, visitors were greeted and beheadings were held. It opens into the Second Courtyard (Divan Meydanı) and the Treasury.

> **EAT**
>
> Need a pick-me-up after visiting the palace? Stop by one of the two cafés in the Second Courtyard for light snacks and a cup of hot coffee.

2 First Courtyard (Alay Meydanı)

This outer courtyard takes in Gülhane Park, the church of Haghia Eirene (Aya İrini Kilisesi, p71) and the famous Archaeological Museum (p30).

4 Treasury (Hazine Koğuşu)

With exhibits such as the bejewelled Topkapı Dagger and the

Gold Topkapı Dagger (1741) in the Treasury

86-carat Spoonmaker's Diamond, the Treasury may be the most ostentatious collection of wealth ever gathered outside of the legendary Aladdin's cave. You'll also find a magnificent assortment of arms and armour here, spanning 1,300 years and sourced from all over the world.

Imperial Hall, the largest room in the Harem

5 Imperial Wardrobe (Seferli Koğuşu)

The Imperial Wardrobe houses the Costume Museum, a collection of some 3,000 royal robes. Look out for the gold-plated inscriptions above the entrance.

6 Throne Room (Arz Odası)

In the Throne Room, the sultan consulted his ministers and governors, welcomed ambassadors and other dignitaries and hosted smaller state occasions.

7 Kitchens

These huge kitchens once catered to more than 1,000 people a day. On display is a collection of ceramics, crystal and silver, including the Chinese celadon ware (green ware) favoured by early sultans.

8 Third Courtyard (Enderûn Meydanı)

The Gate of Felicity (Bâb-üş Saadet) leads to the Third Courtyard, containing the sultan's private quarters and those of the Harem's white eunuchs.

9 Imperial Sofa (Sofa-ı-Hümayun)

The Imperial Sofa was a place to relax, its charming gardens studded with pools and pavilions built by successive sultans. The finest kiosk is the Baghdad Pavilion (Bağdat Köşkü).

Topkapı Palace Site Plan

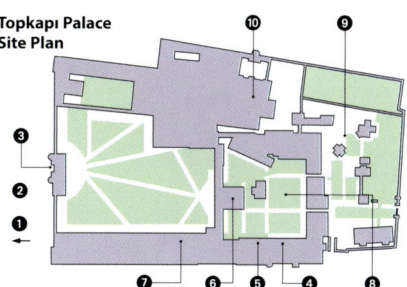

TOP TIP

Expect long queues at the Pavilion of the Holy Mantle and the Treasury.

10 Harem

A maze of more than 300 rooms and corridors, the Harem was a closed world occupied by the sultan's wives, concubines and children. It also housed nine bath-houses and two mosques.

RELIGIOUS RELICS

The Pavilion of the Holy Mantle (Has Oda Koğuşu) contains some of Islam's holiest relics. Exhibits include hairs from the Prophet's beard, one of his teeth, two of his swords and the sacred standard used during his military campaigns. The most important relic of all is the Holy Mantle, a camel-hair cloak that the Prophet gave as a present to a poet. Once a year, this cloak was doused in water; the drops squeezed from it were sent out as talismans against the plague.

Baghdad Pavilion, in the Imperial Sofa

Features of the Topkapı Harem

**Courtyard in the Salon of
the Valide Sultan**

1. Barracks of the Black Eunuchs
Apart from the sultan and his sons, the only men allowed into the Harem were the African eunuchs, up to 200 enslaved people from Sudan and Ethiopia. Their barracks lie on one side of the Courtyard of the Black Eunuchs, with its arcade of marble columns.

2. Courtyard of the Concubines
This striking, colonnaded courtyard lies beside the Harem Baths. As many as 300 concubines lived in the Harem at any one time.

3. Golden Cage
Mehmet III became sultan in 1595 following the murder of all but one of his 19 brothers. After that, heirs to the throne were confined in the "Golden Cage", a secure area of the Harem. As a result, many were weak and ill-fitted for rule when they took the throne.

4. Wives' Apartments
The sultan's wives (under Islamic law, he was allowed four) also had their own apartments. While wives took formal precedence in the Harem hierarchy, the real power lay with the sultan's favourites and mother. Occasionally, a sultan would marry a concubine – as in the case of Süleyman I, who married his beloved Roxelana (known thereafter as Hürrem Sultan).

5. Salon of the Valide Sultan
The *valide sultan* (sultan's mother) was by far the most powerful woman in the palace, and she enjoyed the use of some of the best rooms in the Harem.

6. Sultan's Apartments
The sultan spent much of his off-duty time in his suite within the Harem. Look out for the bedroom of Sultan Abdül Hamit I (1774–89), the Hall of Murat III (1574–95) and the Fruit Room, which is decorated with paintings of pomegranates and pears.

7. Imperial Hammam
At the centre of the complex are the elegant marble baths of the sultan and the *valide sultan*.

8. Imperial Hall
The sultan entertained his closest aides in this hall. Although it was within the Harem, only a few women – the sultan's mother, chief wife, favourites and daughters – were allowed entry.

9. Favourites' Apartments
Haseki (favourites) who bore a child received their own apartments and freedom (if enslaved). After the sultan's death, those who had borne only daughters were moved to the old palace or married out of the Harem; those with sons stayed in the palace.

10. Golden Way
This long, dark passage was so called because, on festivals, the sultan would scatter gold coins here for the members of the Harem.

LIFE IN THE HAREM

**Portrait of
Princess Mihrimah**

Behind the closed doors of the Harem, life was far less exciting than portrayed in the breathless accounts of 19th-century European commentators. There was undoubtedly intrigue and, if a woman was one of the sultan's favourites, she might well develop a taste for lavish comfort and lovely gifts, yet daily existence for most was mundane – even dully routine. The Harem was less a den of vice than a family home and girls' school. Of its 1,000 or so occupants, more than two-thirds were servants or royal children, while concubines – who usually arrived between the ages of five and 12 – spent many years living in dormitories and undergoing a thorough education before being introduced to the sultan. The Harem was not completely removed from politics, though; some women (such as Kösem Sultan and Hürrem Sultan) wielded significant power, influencing political decisions and advising the sultan.

The Topkapı Harem, illustrated in the *Le Tour du Monde* journal (1863)

AYASOFYA (HAGHIA SOPHIA)

📍 R4 | 🏛 Sultanahmet Meydanı | 🕐 8am–7pm daily | 🌐 ayasofyacamii.gov.tr | ↗

One of the oldest symbols of Istanbul, Ayasofya was built as a church in 537 by Emperor Justinian. This impressive structure was converted into a mosque in the 15th century by Mehmet II. From 1935 until 2020 it served as a museum. Today, it's a mosque again, with the nave and inner narthex reserved for worship and the upper galleries open to tourists.

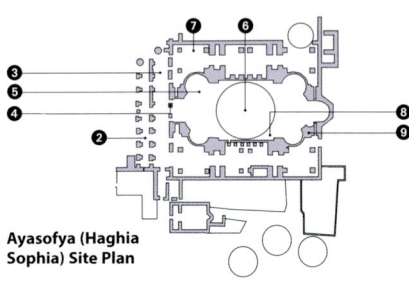

Ayasofya (Haghia Sophia) Site Plan

1 Exterior
The deep-red walls of the exterior are topped by a central dome and flanked by two semi-domes. The main building is as it was in the 6th century – except for the buttresses added to secure the structure, which obscure the shape.

2 Galleries
Women used the galleries on the upper floors for prayer. Votive mosaics adorn their walls; the south gallery features mosaics of Jesus Christ flanked by Empress Zoë and Emperor Constantine IX Monomachus, and Christ Pantocrator (Almighty) with John the Baptist and the Virgin Mary.

3 Inner Narthex
There are doors leading into the nave from each bay of the inner narthex; the large central one, the Imperial Gate, was once reserved for the emperor and the patriarch. As you exit the galleries at the south end of the inner narthex, look back above the door to see the wonderful late 10th-century mosaic of Constantine and Justinian offering their city to the infant Christ.

4 Emperor Door
This massive oak-panelled door was exclusively used by Byzantine emperors, hence the name. Legend has it that its wood is from Noah's Ark, having found its way here from a 2nd-century Tarsun pagan temple.

5 Nave
Looking down into the nave, the overwhelming impression is of the

Ayasofya, Istanbul's most famous monument

Dome with Qur'anic inscriptions in the nave

vast space enclosed by the dome. This sits on four arches rising out of four enormous marble piers, which frame double colonnades at either end.

6 Dome
Ayasofya's massive dome, 32 m (101 ft) in diameter, rises 56 m (183 ft) above the ground. Supported by 40 ribs made from lightweight hollow bricks, it is a miracle of engineering. The original design

DRINK
After your visit, head to Divanyolu Caddesi (p70), which is a short walk from the mosque, and grab a drink in one of its rooftop bars.

survived for 21 years before being destroyed by an earthquake in 1558.

7 Weeping Pillar
Emperor Justinian rested his aching head against the damp stone of this pillar and was instantly cured. Ever since, visitors have queued to touch the miraculous spot.

8 Coronation Square
Set into the floor near the *minbar*, the site of the emperor's throne is marked in a square of patterned marble. In Byzantine times, this was thought to be the centre of the world (*omphalion*).

9 Columns
The Byzantines were prolific scavengers, and a number of the columns in Ayasofya were probably salvaged from pagan temples.

10 Islamic Elements
The conversion of this structure from church to mosque began in 1453. Many of the mosaics were plastered over, to be rediscovered in the 1930s. The *mihrab* and *minbar (p29)* were added by Sultan Murat III in the 16th century. Note the calligraphic roundels at the dome base.

CHANGING FACES

In the last bay of the south gallery, look for the mosaic of Christ enthroned, flanked by Empress Zoë and Emperor Constantine IX Monomachus. Historians believe that the figure of the emperor was initially Zoë's first husband, Romanos III Argyros, but that was replaced with the image of her second husband, Michael IV, then the face of her third husband, Constantine.

BLUE MOSQUE

📍 R5 📍 Sultanahmet Meydanı 📞 (0212) 458 49 83 🕐 9am–7pm daily
🕐 Prayer times

Sultan Ahmet I was only 19 when he commissioned this mosque, known in Turkish as Sultanahmet Camii. With his architect, Sedefkar Mehmet Ağa, he wanted to surpass Ayasofya (Haghia Sophia) and the Süleymaniye Mosque Complex. The result, completed in 1616, has become one of the most celebrated mosques in the world, widely known as the Blue Mosque because of the blue İznik tiles inside.

1 The Setting
To underline the supremacy of Islam over Christian Byzantium, the Blue Mosque was built opposite Ayasofya, on the site of the former Byzantine royal palace.

2 Entrance
The mosque's main entrance can only be accessed by practising Muslims. There are separate entrances for visitors of other faiths around the side of the mosque.

3 Minarets
Legend has it that the sultan asked for a minaret with *altın* (gold), but the architect heard *altı* (six) minarets. The sultan was still pleased with the result – at that time, no mosque apart from the great mosque in Mecca had six minarets.

4 Domes
The mosque's central dome is 23.5 m (77 ft) in diameter and 43 m (140 ft) high, and supported by four giant columns, each 5 m (16 ft) in diameter. This main dome is in turn surrounded by smaller, cascading semi-domes, instilling the structure

TOP TIP

Visit at night to see both Ayasofya *(p26)* and the Blue Mosque floodlit.

Clockwise from below **Inside the prayer hall; central dome decorated with blue İznik tiles; Ablutions Fountain in the courtyard; detail on an İznik tile**

The Blue Mosque rising above the Sea of Marmara

with an overwhelming splendour and majesty.

5 Courtyard
The expansive courtyard, which is faced with cool marble from Marmara island, has the same dimensions as the interior of the prayer hall. Look up for a splendid view of the mosque's cascade of domes and semi-domes.

6 Ablutions Fountain
The fountain at the centre of the mosque's courtyard was originally used for ritual ablutions. Today, the faithful use taps ranged along the outside of the courtyard. Washing one's face, arms, neck, feet, mouth and nose is seen as an integral part of the act of prayer.

7 Minbar and Mihrab
The *minbar* and *mihrab* – characteristic features of all mosques – are located at the front. The *minbar*,

the pulpit from which the imam delivers his sermons, is positioned so that the imam can be heard from anywhere in the mosque. The *mihrab*, which is a niche that points towards Mecca, is made of carved marble.

8 Sultan's Loge
To the left of the *mihrab* is the galleried box where the sultan prayed. The interior is decorated with stained-glass windows and the ceiling is painted with arabesque designs.

9 Carpets
The interior of the mosque is laid with a modern carpet. Mosques have always had carpets in order to cushion the knees and forehead during prayer time.

10 Tiles
There are more than 20,000 blue İznik tiles lining the mosque's interior walls. Supplying these tiles put severe pressure on the tile

makers, and the sultan banned anyone else from placing orders until the mosque was completed.

İZNIK TILES
Ceramic production in İznik began during the Byzantine era. Initially, the designs were based on Chinese models. Arabic motifs were added by Şahkulu, one of 16 artists brought in from Tabriz by Sultan Selim I (1512–20). A rich turquoise was added to the traditional blue and white in the 1530s; purples, greens and coral reds came 20 years later. Master designer Kara Memi introduced swirling floral patterns. By the time Ahmet I commissioned the Blue Mosque, the İznik style was established.

ARCHAEOLOGICAL MUSEUM

📍 S3   🏛 Osman Hamdi Bey Yokuşu, Gülhane Parkı   🕐 9am–9pm daily (last adm: 8pm)   🌐 muze.gov.tr ↗

Home to a world-class collection spanning 5,000 years, the Archaeological Museum was founded in 1881 by Osman Hamdi Bey, the son of a grand vizier, fuelled by the realization that European archaeologists and treasure hunters were walking off with much of the Empire's heritage. There are three sections: the main museum; the Tiled Pavilion (Çinili Köşk) and the Museum of the Ancient Orient.

ANCIENT WELCOME

In the entrance hall to the main museum stands a statue of the Egyptian god Bes. At the foot of the stairs to the Museum of the Ancient Orient are two basalt lions from Samal, dating from the 8th century BCE. Outside the main museum are porphyry sarcophagi, from the 4th–5th century CE. The portico itself is modelled on the 4th-century-BCE Sarcophagus of the Mourning Women.

1 Alexander Sarcophagus

Though its frieze depicts Alexander battling the Persians, the Alexander Sarcophagus, dating from the late 4th century BCE, is in fact the tomb of King Abdalonymos of Sidon (died c 312 BCE). Faint traces remain of the gaudy colour that would once have covered it.

2 Halikarnassos Lion

The tomb of King Mausolus was one of the Seven Wonders of the Ancient World – this lion is a surviving relic.

3 Sidon Sarcophagi

Osman Hamdi Bey discovered this remarkable group of 5th- and 4th-century-BCE sarcophagi in Sidon (modern-day Lebanon) in 1887. These coffins are made of Parian

Intricately carved Sidon sarcophagus

Roman sculptures on display in the museum

marble. Intricate reliefs on the sides depict mythical creatures and hunting scenes.

4 Hattuşa Sphinx
This stone feline, dating from 13th century BCE, was one of four discovered in the great Hittite city at Hattuşa (Boğazkale) in Anatolia.

5 Treaty of Kadesh
The oldest surviving peace treaty in the world, carved in stone in 1269 BCE, was agreed on by Egyptian Pharaoh Ramses II and King Hattusilis III of the Hittites after a battle in present-day Syria. It lays out the terms of the ceasefire and agrees the safe return of refugees.

6 Ishtar Gate
The Ishtar Gate, built by King Nebuchadnezzar II in 575 BCE, was decorated with ceramic brick panels of dragons and bulls. The Processional Way through the gate was lined with 120 lions.

7 Hellenistic and Roman Sculptures
An array of beautiful larger-than-life statues of goddesses, gods and emperors can be seen in the museum. Notable are the remains of an Aphrodisian frieze, which depicts the epic battle between the Olympian gods and giants.

8 Troy Gallery
The fascinating history of the ancient city of Troy is recounted in this gallery. The focal point is a floor-to-ceiling, rammed-earth replica of the archaeological layers uncovered at its site.

Glazed frieze of a lion, Ishtar Gate

9 Museum of the Ancient Orient
⟳ For renovation till 2026
This museum houses exhibits from Babylon, Mesopotamia and Egypt, including some of the world's first known writing – cuneiform clay tablets from 2700 BCE.

10 Tiled Pavilion
⟳ For renovation until 2026
Istanbul's oldest secular building (1472) tells the story of Turkish ceramics, with displays from İznik and Kütahya.

Key to Floorplan
- 🟪 Third floor
- 🟨 Second floor
- 🟥 First floor
- 🟩 Ground floor

Archaeological Museum Floorplan

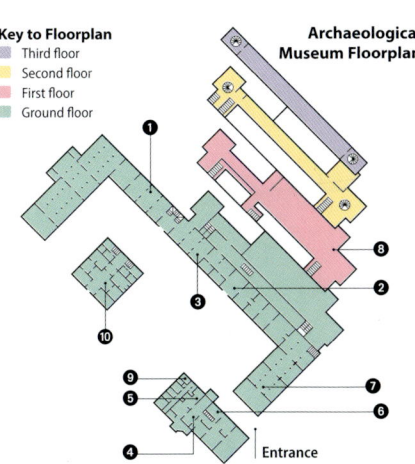

GRAND BAZAAR

🅿 N3 📞 (0212) 519 12 48 🕐 9am–7pm Mon–Sat (surrounding street markets are usually open longer and also on Sun)

From the painted arches to the shopfronts gleaming with lanterns, piled with carpets or heaped with spices, the Grand Bazaar (Kapalı Çarşı) is a fantasy of Eastern opulence. Founded in 1461 by Sultan Mehmet II, the bazaar was designed as the trading heart of an empire. Today, its many shops and cafés offer an entertaining day out.

EAT
There are a number of small tea and coffee shops scattered throughout the market, as well as good kebab stalls and a range of upmarket cafés.

1 İç Bedesten
This covered market hall was the bazaar's first building – a Byzantine structure converted in 1461 into a sturdy lock-up in which jewellery was traded and enslaved people were auctioned. Today, it houses more than 120 shops selling precious goods such as antiques and rare icons.

2 Sandal Bedesten
In the southeast corner of the market, the 15th-century Sandal Bedesten is the second-oldest part of the bazaar. The roof of its arcade consists of 20 brick domes propped up by pillars. It is the former antiques market.

3 Jewellers' Street (Kalpakçılar Caddesi)
The bazaar's widest street runs along the southern edge of the market, its shop windows piled high with jewels

Ottoman-style bracelet, Jewellers' Street

and precious metals. Some 100,000 kg (220,460 lb) of gold is traded in the bazaar each year. Gold jewellery is sold by weight.

4 Zincirli Han
The *hans* provided accommodation, food and stables for travelling traders. This intimate *han*, the oldest of 40 in the area, has been

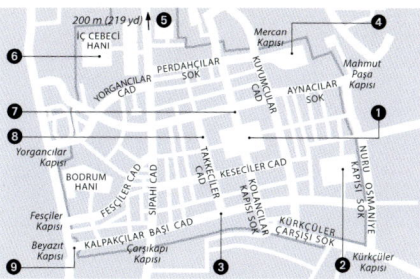

Beautiful carpets for sale in the bazaar

lovingly restored and is occupied by Şişko Osman, a leading carpet dealer.

5 Büyük Valide Han

Located on Çakmakçılar Yokuşu, this huge building, constructed in 1651, has been sadly neglected. Today, it contains a mix of residential, gallery and workshop space.

6 Artisans' Courtyard (İç Cebeci Han)

Deep inside the bazaar, off Yağlıkçılar Sok, is an 18th-century courtyard

that seems like a window into a bygone era. Here, artisans still practise their trades in the same way they have for hundreds of years. It's a tranquil space away from the hubbub of the main market.

7 Carpet Sellers

The bazaar is home to Istanbul's finest carpet dealers and lesser traders keen to sell you a hall runner or a bedside rug. Shops are scattered all over the market, especially on Halıcılar Caddesi and near the İç Bedesten.

8 Fountains

Two marble and copper fountains provided drinking water for the market traders before modern plumbing was installed. An 1880 survey noted there were also 16 drinking-water posts, one fountain reservoir and eight wells for firefighters.

9 Gates

Twenty-two gates provide entry into the covered bazaar from all

Shop selling colourful wares in the İç Bedesten

directions. The Beyazıt Gate, rebuilt after an earthquake in 1894, is marked with the *tuğra* (imperial sign) of Sultan Abdül Hamit II and the assurance that "God loves tradesmen".

10 Outdoor Stalls

Surrounding the covered market is a maze of tiny lanes, with stalls selling carpets, souvenirs, clothes and homewares. These stalls are very popular with locals.

IN NUMBERS

In business since its foundation in 1461, the Grand Bazaar is the world's oldest covered market. It contains a network of 61 covered streets, enclosing an area of 307,000 sq m (3,305,000 sq ft). Every day, as many as 30,000 traders in 4,500 shops befriend and haggle with up to 400,000 shoppers (both locals and visitors from all around the world).

SÜLEYMANIYE MOSQUE COMPLEX

🗺 M2 🏛 Prof Sıddık Sami Onar Cad 📞 (0212) 458 00 00 🕐 8:30am–4:45pm daily 🕌 Prayer times

One of the finest creations of the Ottoman Empire's greatest architect, Sinan, Süleymaniye Camii was built in 1550–57 for Süleyman I. The mosque's dome and minarets dominate the skyline, while its stained-glass windows and lovely carvings add a lightness of touch. The tombs of Süleyman and his wife Hürrem Sultan are also housed here.

1 Mosque Interior
The interior is simple and serene. The blue, white and gold dome contains 200 stained-glass windows. The *mihrab* and pulpit are made from white marble with İznik tiles.

2 Süleyman's Tomb
🕐 9am–5pm daily
Sultan Süleyman I, "the Magnificent", lies in a grandiose tomb surrounded by lush gardens. The tomb has an ebony, mother-of-pearl and ivory door and a dome inlaid with ceramic stars.

3 Sinan's Tomb
🕐 9am–5pm daily
Sinan's mausoleum is on the site of the house he lived in when he was building the mosque, just beyond the northwest corner of the complex. It is a modest memorial to a prodigious talent.

4 Courtyard
This great courtyard is surrounded by a colonnade of pink Egyptian,

Ornate interior of the mosque's dome

The splendid Süleymaniye Mosque Complex

> 🍴 **EAT**
> Lalezar Café
> *(543 541 37 59)* on
> İsmetiye Cad and
> Mimar Sinan Roof
> *(mimarsinanroof.
> com.tr)* on Fetva
> Yokuş offer great
> snacks and hookah.

Marmara and porphyry columns, recycled from the Hippodrome.

5 Hammam
⏰ 10am–9:30pm daily (last adm: 8pm); men only 6–10am Mon–Sat 🌐 suleyman iyehamami.com.tr 🔑 The hammam in this mosque is a mixed-sex bathhouse, which makes it especially good for families. Sultan Süleyman was a frequent visitor to the bathhouse.

6 Caravanserai
The mosque was a full-service complex in the past – at the *caravanserai* (inn), visitors could find food and convenient lodging.

7 Medreses
Two of the six *medreses* – colleges that were once part of the Imperial religious school providing theological and general education – house Süleyman's library of 110,000 manuscripts.

8 İmaret
The mosque kitchens not only fed the many teachers, students, workers and priests in the complex, but also ran a soup kitchen for up to 1,000 people a day.

9 Views
The terraced gardens outside the

The mosque's domes, set against the city's skyline

main complex offer superb views across the Golden Horn.

10 Addicts' Alley
The cafés of "Addicts' Alley", formally known as Prof Sıddık Sami Onar Caddesi, once sold opium and hashish. This street is still lined with cafés, but now the "drug" of choice is tobacco smoked in a *nargile* (water pipe).

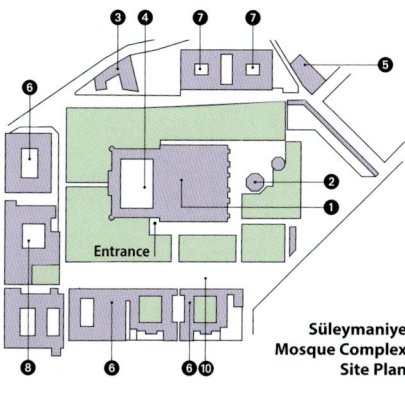

Süleymaniye Mosque Complex Site Plan

KARIYE MOSQUE

📍 B2 🏛 Kariye Camii Sok, Kariye Meydanı, Edirnekapı ⏰ 9am–6pm Sat–Thu 🌐 hariyecamii.com

Formerly the Church of St Saviour in Chora, Kariye Mosque (Kariye Camii) has one of the world's finest collections of Byzantine art, commissioned between 1315 and 1321 by statesman Theodore Metochites. The church was converted into a mosque in 1511 and its artworks slipped into obscurity until their rediscovery in 1860. The nave is now reserved for male Muslim worshippers and is off-limits to other visitors.

1 Exterior

Walk round the back of the building to experience the full impact of its architecture – masonry of striped marble, six domes, layers of arches, undulating rooflines and, to one side, a minaret.

2 Genealogy of Christ

The two domes of the inner narthex (western entrance) portray 66 of Christ's forebears. In one dome, the Virgin and Child survey the kings of the House of David. In the other, Christ is surrounded by ancestors, including Abraham, Adam, Jacob and Jacob's 12 sons.

3 Ministry of Christ

The south bay of the inner narthex and the seven bays in the outer narthex detail the ministry of Christ, including his temptation and the miracles he performed.

4 Life of the Virgin

Twenty mosaics in the first three bays of the inner narthex depict the life of the Virgin Mary. These mosaics are based on the apocryphal 2nd-century Gospel of St James. They include images of Mary's first steps (at six months old).

> 🍴 **EAT**
> The tea garden in front of Kariye Mosque is a peaceful place to take a break. Sip on Turkish tea as you take in views of the old city walls.

Clockwise from below Dormition of the Virgin mosaic in the nave; Byzantine frescoes lining the mosque's ceiling; the Kariye Mosque complex

5 Pareclesion

In the complex's southern portion is a chapel once used for burials and funerals. Its walls are adorned with frescoes depicting judgment and resurrection. The unmarked tomb in the north wall is believed to be that of Theodore Metochites.

6 The Last Judgment

In the main dome of the Pareclesion is a vision of the Last Judgment, with Christ in Majesty flanked by the Virgin Mary, John the Baptist and the Apostles.

7 Anastasis Fresco

Also housed in the Pareclesion, this Resurrection fresco depicts Christ pulling Adam and Eve from their graves, while the gates of hell are broken and Satan lies bound at Christ's feet.

8 Dormition of the Virgin

This beautiful mosaic in the nave portrays

Virgin and Child with Angels, Pareclesion

Christ sitting beside his mother's coffin, cradling a baby that represents her soul. Above is Ashrael, the Angel of Death.

9 Mosaic of Theodore Metochites

Over the door leading from the inner narthex to the nave is an exquisite mosaic depicting Theodore Metochites in a large turban presenting a model of the Chora to Christ. Christ is shown seated on a jewelled throne, raising a hand in blessing.

10 Infancy of Christ

Scenes from Christ's infancy are depicted in the semicircular panels of the outer narthex. Based on New Testament accounts, they include the Journey to Bethlehem, Mary and Joseph enrolling for taxation, the Nativity, and the terrible Massacre of the Innocents.

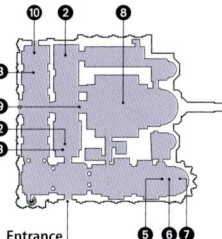

Kariye Mosque Site Plan

✛ MOSQUE GUIDE

You can enter via a side door, but originally entry was by way of a long porch, the outer narthex, which leads into an inner narthex. Most of the mosaics line the ceilings and walls of the narthexes. The inner narthex opens into what was once the nave. The altar at the far end is flanked by the Diakonikon (vestry), and the Prothesis (Communion chapel). On the south side is the Pareclesion (funerary chapel).

ÇEMBERLITAŞ HAMMAM

⊙ P4 ⌂ Vezirhan Cad 8 ⏱ 6am–midnight daily ⓦ cemberlitas hamami.com ↗

No stay in Istanbul would be complete without a bout of steaming, soaping, scrubbing and massaging in a hammam (Turkish bath). Çemberlitaş, built in 1584, is hailed as one of the most beautiful. Designed by Sinan, it was commissioned by Selim II's wife, Nurbanu Sultan, as a way of providing financial support for the Atik Valide Sultan Mosque in Üsküdar. Today, Çemberlitaş is still used by Turks but is most popular with tourists and photographers.

Çemberlitaş Hammam Floorplan

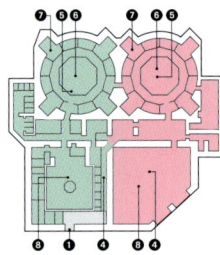

Key to Floorplan
🟩 Men's section
🟥 Women's section

1 Entrance
There is an inscription decorated with rumi motifs over the entrance door. At the ticket office, you are given a *peştemal*, a type of sarong, for modesty, a *kese,* a coarse mitt for scrubbing the body, and tokens to give to the attendants. Men and women are then sent off to separate sections.

2 Men's Section
The hammam originally consisted of two identical suites, each with a separate entrance. The men's section of the hammam, entered via Vezir Hanı Caddesi, is still exactly as envisaged by its creator, Sinan.

3 Women's Section
The women's changing area was lost in 1868, when Divanyolu Caddesi was widened, so women now change in a corridor; but their hot room remains unaltered.

Wooden cabins in the men's dressing room

modern. Afterwards, head back to change, or go for your oil massage.

9 Oil Massage Rooms

You will be one of several people being massaged on a row of beds under bright lights. Fragrant plant-based oils are used for the massage. It's worth any discomfort you may experience – you'll feel great afterwards.

4 Dressing Rooms (Camekan)

In the dressing rooms, an attendant will assign you a locker and give you a pair of slippers. Most people go nude under the *peştemal*, but wear a swimsuit if you wish to. These chambers also have a common lounge space for socializing.

5 Hot Rooms (Sıcaklık)

Both hot rooms have a domed ceiling supported by 12 arches that rise from marble columns. The dome is pitted with glass "elephants' eyes", which channel the light through the steam to polka-dot the floor.

TOP TIP

The heat in the hammam can dehydrate you, so carry a bottle of water.

Enjoying a steamed bath in the hot room

6 Navel Stones (Göbek Taşı)

In the centre of the hot rooms is a large slab of marble. Lie down and wait for the attendant. You will be covered in soap suds and scrubbed all over with the *kese*. Then you will be lathered again, washed with a cloth and massaged with soap. Finally, your hair will be washed, and you will be vigorously rinsed with buckets of water.

7 Bathing Alcoves (Halvets)

Around the walls of the hot rooms are a number of small cubicles. They have taps running cold, warm and hot water, which you can use to wash or cool down if the heat and steam get too much for you.

8 Cool Rooms (Soğukluk)

The cool rooms provide a place to sit and chat. The men's is as elegant as it was in Sinan's day; the women's is more

10 Extras

Take as much time as you like to return to the steam room or sit in the cool room. If you want the full works, the attendants will be happy to give you a manicure, pedicure or facial.

ANCIENT CUSTOMS

The direct descendant of the Graeco-Roman bath, the hammam was eagerly adopted by Islamic invaders who really did believe that cleanliness is next to godliness. The hammam became a place not only to cleanse and detoxify the body, but also to restore the spirit. For women, time in the hammam was a welcome escape from the narrow world of their daily lives, as well as a place for them to find potential daughters-in-law.

DOLMABAHÇE PALACE

📍 H1 🏠 Dolmabahçe Cad 🕐 For tours: 9am–5:30pm Tue–Sun
🌐 millisaraylar.gov.tr 🔲🔲

In 1843, Sultan Abdül Mecit employed Armenian architects Garabet and Nikoğos Balyan to build a luxurious palace on the Bosphorus shore. Dolmabahçe Sarayı, completed in 1856, is the result. Luxurious it certainly is, with 285 rooms and 43 halls, and crystal and gold detailing that rivals the Palace of Versailles in France. Ironically, this opulence hastened the end of the Empire, and the last sultan fled from here in 1922.

1 Waterfront Façade
The impressive marble façade of Dolmabahçe Palace is 284 m (930 ft) long and glitters on the banks of the Bosphorus. The State Rooms are on the left, the Harem on the right and the Ceremonial Hall in the centre.

EAT
The café next to the Cloch Tower overlooks the palatial gardens and the Bosphorus. Grab an outdoor table here at sunset for a memorable experience.

2 Gates
The palace had two ceremonial entrances, both highly ornamented: the Treasury Gate, which is now the main entrance, and the Imperial Gate. Both gates still have a guard of honour.

3 Ceremonial Hall (Muayede Salonu)
The dome in this vast hall is 36 m (118 ft) high. The Bohemian crystal chandelier, a gift from Queen Victoria of the UK, has 750 lights and weighs 4.5 tonnes (9,900 lb). It is the world's largest such chandelier.

4 Harem
The apartments in the Harem are furnished to various grades of luxury (for the sultan, his mother, wives, concubines, servants and guests). The vast complex includes a school, a hammam, a maternity ward and a spacious central salon where the concubines and wives would meet for tea.

5 Atatürk's Rooms
In the first years of the republic, Atatürk used the palace as his Istanbul base, keeping an office and bedroom in the

Imperial Gate, the main entrance to the palace

7 State Rooms (Selamlık)

The lavish rooms on the palace's seaward side were used by the grand vizier and ministers, while those on the landward side were administrative offices.

8 Crystal Staircase

This ornate staircase has balusters of Baccarat crystal. It links the administrative offices with the ceremonial rooms upstairs.

9 Clock Tower

The four-storey tower, 27 m (90 ft) high, was added to the palace in 1890, during the reign of Sultan Abdül Hamit II (*p97*). The clock – which still keeps time – was built by the celebrated Parisian clockmaker Paul Garnier.

ATATÜRK

Mustafa Kemal (1881–1938) rose to power in 1915, leading Turkish forces to victory at Gallipoli. A leader of the Young Turks movement, he seized his moment after the end of World War I, abolishing the sultanate in 1922. As Turkey's first president, he introduced the Latin alphabet, compulsory schooling and rights for women. He is still idolized as the "Father of the Turks" (Atatürk); it is illegal in Turkey to criticize him publicly.

10 Gardens

The palace stands on reclaimed land that was converted into a beautiful garden (the name Dolmabahçe means "Filled Garden").

Harem. He died here, from cirrhosis of the liver, on 10 November 1938 – all the palace's clocks are set to 9:05am, the moment of his death.

6 Sultan's Bathrooms

The sultan had two bathrooms: one in the main palace, faced in marble; the other in the Harem, decorated in violet flowers.

Clockwise from right
Crystal chandelier in the Ceremonial Hall; double-horseshoe Crystal Staircase; Clock Tower in the palace grounds; waterfront façade of the palace

BOSPHORUS CRUISE

📍 F4 🏛 Eminönü Boğaz Hattı Pier 🕐 Long cruise: 10:35am daily; short cruise: 2:40pm daily 🌐 sehirhatlari.istanbul ♿

The Istanbul skyline is justifiably one of the most famous cityscapes in the world, and while there are many places from which to admire it, by far the best is the deck of a boat on the Bosphorus. Take the local ferry for a modest fare, and spend a day floating serenely along the straits past magnificent shores and wooden villas.

1 Eminönü Pier
The Bosphorus ferry departs from Eminönü port, the city's busiest ferry terminal. Pick up a simit (p57) or a fish sandwich from a street vendor here.

2 Maiden's Tower (Kız Kulesi)
This tower (p101), off the Üsküdar shore, has a small café inside. Its Turkish name refers to a legendary princess who was supposedly confined here; its English name is "Leander's Tower", after a hero of Greek myth.

3 Dolmabahçe Palace (Dolmabahçe Sarayı)
Sultan Abdül Mecit II virtually mortgaged the Ottoman Empire to build this extravagant, European-style palace (p40) in the 1850s.

4 Ortaköy
With a Baroque mosque at the foot of the bridge, as well as a range of swanky

Ortaköy's fashionable waterfront

restaurants, Ortaköy (p98) is a popular spot for a weekend stroll.

5 15th July Martyrs' Bridge (15 Temmuz Şehitler Köprüsü)
Straddling Europe and Asia, this bridge (p42) is a symbol of national unity.

TOP TIP

A one-way cruise departs from Eminönü Pier to the 15th July Martyrs' Bridge.

Enjoying a cruise on the Bosphorus

It is 1,510 m (4,954 ft) long and was the first to link the two continents. Its name is a tribute to the 34 people who died here during the failed military coup in 2016.

IT'S ALL A MYTH

When Greek goddess Hera sent a swarm of gnats to plague Io, her rival for the affections of the god Zeus, Io turned herself into a cow and swam across the straits to escape, giving the Bosphorus its name – the "Ford of the Cow". In another Greek myth, Jason and the Argonauts rowed up the Bosphorus in search of the Golden Fleece – perhaps an echo of the Black Sea tradition of using a lamb's fleece to trap gold when panning.

6 Beylerbeyi Palace (Asian Side) (Beylerbeyi Sarayı)

This palace *(p95)* was built in 1860–65 as a summer annexe to the Dolmabahçe *(p40)*. It had no kitchens, and food was rowed across as required.

7 Arnavutköy and Bebek

The neighbourhoods of Arnavutköy *(p98)* and Bebek extend along the central stretch of the Bosphorus. The pretty 19th-century wooden *yalıs* (villas) that line the waterfront here are some of the city's most desirable real estate.

8 Fortress of Europe (Rumeli Hisarı)

This vast castle *(p96)* was built by Mehmet II in 1452 prior to his attack on Constantinople. Just across the water stands the smaller (but equally impressive) Fortress of Asia (Anadolu Hisarı, *p98*), built in the late 14th century.

9 Sarıyer

This village is the main fishing port on the Bosphorus. It has a historic fish market, as well as several good fish restaurants near the shore.

10 Anadolu Kavağı (Asian Side)

This is the last stop for the ferry, and the locals make a good living selling fish lunches and ice cream to tourists. The 14th-century Yoros Kalesi here offers good views. The return cruise takes six hours and includes a stop in Anadolu Kavağı for two-and-a-half hours.

Fortress of Europe overlooking the Bosphorus

TOP 10 OF EVERYTHING

A glass of traditional Turkish tea

MUSEUMS AND GALLERIES

1 Istanbul Modern
For centuries, Turkish art was better known for tradition rather than innovation, but an increasing number of contemporary Turkish artists are exploring new avenues. Set in Galataport, a hub of culture, art and design in Karaköy, Istanbul Modern *(p95)* is an ideal platform for showcasing art from the 19th to the 21st centuries.

2 Topkapı Palace (Topkapı Sarayı)
The buildings in this complex *(p22)* are spectacular, and some of the collections are even more so – from the sea of beautiful Chinese porcelain in the kitchens to the four-room Treasury, with its display of priceless jewellery, intricately carved ivory heirlooms and great rocks of emerald. Religious treasures on display include hair from the Prophet's beard.

Impressive façade of the Naval Museum

3 Naval Museum (Deniz Müzesi)
For centuries, the Ottoman navy ruled the seas, and its achievements are celebrated here *(p95)*. This marvellous museum was originally established in 1897. Among the exhibits are figureheads and engravings, but the flamboyantly decorated royal barges, which include *caïques* and galleys, are the highlights of any visit.

4 Military Museum (Askeri Müze)
Among the fascinating exhibits at this museum *(p88)* are *cembiyes* (curved daggers), carried by 15th-century Ottoman foot soldiers, and the vast imperial tents used by sultans during their military campaigns. The Mehter Band, founded in the 14th century, plays Ottoman military music daily at 3pm.

5 Pera Museum (Pera Müzesi)
The privately-run Pera Museum *(p89)* houses an intriguing mix of fine art, such as Vanmour's *Women Drinking Coffee*, modern exhibitions and ancient weights and measures.

6 Sakıp Sabancı Museum (Sakıp Sabancı Müzesi)
Known locally as the "Horse Mansion", this engaging museum *(p96)* houses

Chinese ceramics and porcelain at the Topkapı Palace

the collection of the late Turkish business tycoon Sakıp Sabancı. The displays encompass 500 years of Ottoman calligraphy and Ottoman and Turkish painting of the 19th and 20th centuries.

7 Museum of Turkish and Islamic Arts (Türk ve İslam Eserleri Müzesi)

This superb collection in the 16th-century palace (p67) of İbrahim Paşa, spans 1,300 years of the finest works of Turkish and Islamic art. Among the exhibits are splendid Turkish carpets, calligraphy and ethnographic items.

8 Rahmi Koç Museum (Rahmi Koç Müzesi)

An Ottoman foundry and nearby shipyard on the Golden Horn are the perfect setting (p82) for this world-class collection of all things mechanical, from vintage cars to model planes – and even a submarine.

9 Sadberk Hanım Museum (Sadberk Hanım Müzesi)

Two lovingly restored Bosphorus mansions (p97) house an inspiring collection of Anatolian artefacts, Ottoman costumes and ceramics.

10 Archaeological Museum (Arkeoloji Müzesi)

The highlight at this museum (p30) is the tomb of Abdalonymus of Sidon, known as the "Alexander Sarcophagus". It depicts Alexander the Great defeating the Persians at the Battle of Issus in 333 BCE.

Abdalonymus's tomb, Archaeological Museum

TOP 10 LESSER-KNOWN MUSEUMS

1. SALT Beyoğlu
This gallery complex (p60) is housed in a restored 19th-century apartment block on busy İstiklal Caddesi (p87).

2. Mevlevi Monastery
Learn about whirling dervishes in this monastery-turned-museum (p88).

3. Barış Manço Evi
⊕ F3 ⌂ Yusuf Kamil Paşa Sok 5, Kadıköy ⓦ barismanco.kadikoy.bel.tr
A lovely house museum dedicated to the beloved Turkish rock musician and TV star Barış Manço.

4. Railway Museum
The *Orient Express* silver service is the star among 300 exhibits on display at this museum in Sirkeci Station (p69).

5. Memory 15 July Museum
Commemorating the resistance to the 2016 coup attempt, this modern museum (p98) sheds light on Turkey's current political scene.

6. Aşiyan Museum
A Bosphorus mansion (p96) pays homage to the city's famous 20th-century poets and thinkers.

7. Museum of the History of Science and Technology in Islam
See displays of historical tools, used in everything from astronomy to war, in this fascinating museum (p71).

8. Museum of Innocence
The Turkish Nobel Prize-winning novelist Orhan Pamuk created this conceptual museum (p88) alongside his book of the same name.

9. Arter
⊕ G1 ⌂ Irmak Cad 13, Dolapdere, Beyoğlu ⓦ arter.org.tr
The Arter cultural centre is known for its contemporary art exhibitions.

10. Atatürk Museum
⊕ T3 ⌂ Halaskargazi Cad 140, Şişli ☎ (0212) 240 63 19
This historic residence is now home to a poignant memorial museum dedicated to Turkey's first president, Mustafa Kemal Atatürk (p41).

BYZANTINE MONUMENTS

1 Ayasofya (Haghia Sophia)
Built by Emperor Justinian in the 6th century, Ayasofya *(p26)* is one of the world's greatest architectural achievements. Justinian was so proud of his basilica that he proclaimed: "Glory to God who has thought me worthy to finish this work. Solomon, I have outdone you".

2 Cisterns
To ensure good water supply in times both of peace and of siege, the Byzantines built a series of vast underground water cisterns beneath their city. The finest are the Basilica Cistern *(p69)* and the Cistern of 1,001 Columns *(p70)*.

3 Theodosian Walls (Teodos II Surları)
🗺 A6
Over the course of 1,000 years, the huge curtain walls built by Emperor Theodosius II from 412 to 422 proved to be a necessity – they withstood more than 20 attacks by Huns, Arabs, Turks, Bulgarians and Russians, finally succumbing to the Ottomans in 1453. The walls have now been partially restored.

4 Hippodrome (At Meydanı)
Once a Byzantine race track 450 m (1,500 ft) long, the Hippodrome *(p67)* could hold 100,000 people. It was the scene of celebrations and, on occasion, bloodshed; the Nika Riots in 532 ended with 30,000 dead.

5 Great Palace Mosaic Museum (Büyük Saray Mozaikleri Müzesi)
Only fragments remain of the Great Palace of the Byzantine emperors. This small museum *(p70)* houses one of them – the lovely mosaic passageway, discovered in the 1930s, that led from the palace to the royal box in the Hippodrome. The floor depicts wild animals and various hunting scenes.

6 Fethiye Mosque (Fethiye Camii)
Constructed in the 12th century, this historic Byzantine building *(p81)* originally served as a church and acted as the worldwide headquarters of the Greek Orthodox faith during the 15th and 16th centuries. It was converted to a mosque in 1573. Note that the mosque's former funerary chapel is not open to visitors as it is undergoing restoration.

Beautiful ceiling frescoes at Kariye Mosque

7 Kariye Mosque (Kariye Camii)

The main reason to visit this striking 11th-century Byzantine church *(p36)* is its glorious collection of mosaics and frescoes, which depict biblical scenes.

8 Church of SS Sergius and Bacchus (Küçük Ayasofya Camii)

In the historic heart of the city, just south of Sultanahmet Square, the Church of SS Sergius and Bacchus *(p71)* was built in the 6th century and has an original Greek frieze.

9 Aqueduct of Valens (Bozdoğan Kemeri)

This beautifully preserved 4th-century aqueduct *(p81)*, which remained in use until the 19th century, was a key part of the system that carried fresh water into the Byzantine capital from the forests of Thrace.

10 Haghia Eirene (Aya İrini Kilisesi)

One of the oldest churches in Istanbul, Haghia Eirene *(p71)* stands in the outer courtyard of the Topkapı Palace. The church was rebuilt in the 6th century and acted as a sister church to the nearby Ayasofya *(p26)*.

Egyptian Obelisk in the centre of the Hippodrome

TOP 10 NOTABLE BYZANTINE RULERS

1. Constantine *(306–37)*
Constantine moved the capital of the Roman Empire from Rome to Constantinople in 330 CE. He began an ambitious programme of construction work in the city, which included the Great Palace and various public buildings.

2. Theodosius II *(408–50)*
Emperor Theodosius codified the law, founded a university and built the city walls *(p48)*.

3. Justinian I *(527–65)*
Justinian founded many great buildings, including Ayasofya *(p26)*, and also reformed the law.

4. Theodora *(527–48)*
A bear-keeper's daughter, Theodora ruled alongside her husband Justinian I until her death.

5. Justinian II *(685–95, 705–11)*
Justinian's enemies deposed him, then cut off his nose, because a disfigured man could not be emperor. He later regained the throne wearing, it is said, a prosthetic nose of solid gold.

6. Irene of Athens *(797–802)*
Irene was the first woman to rule the Empire on her own.

7. Basil I *(867–86)*
Believed to have been in a queer relationship with Michael III, Basil was crowned joint emperor in 866. He later killed Michael to rule alone.

8. Zoë *(1028–50)*
Zoë wed three times after becoming empress aged 50.

9. Romanus IV Diogenes *(1067–71)*
Romanus was defeated by the Seljuks at Manzikert in 1071 and as a result he was exiled.

10. Constantine XI Palaeologus *(1449–53)*
The last of the Byzantines, Constantine XI died fighting on the city walls during the conquest of 1453.

PLACES OF WORSHIP

1 Süleymaniye Mosque Complex (Süleymaniye Camii)

This vast mosque *(p34)*, which dominates the skyline of the Golden Horn, is the crowning achievement of Mimar Sinan, greatest of imperial architects. Built in 1550–57 in the grounds of the old palace, Eski Saray, it is a suitably grand memorial to its founder, Süleyman I *(p69)*.

2 Blue Mosque (Sultanahmet Camii)

Commissioned by Sultan Ahmet I, the magnificent Blue Mosque *(p28)* was built by the imperial architect Sedefkar Mehmet Ağa, a pupil of the great Sinan, in 1609–16. The mosque takes its name from the blue İznik tiles that line its inner walls.

3 Fatih Mosque (Fatih Camii)

The original Fatih Mosque was built by Mehmet II to celebrate his capture of Constantinople in 1453; its name means "the Conqueror's mosque". The present mosque *(p81)* was built in the 18th century by Mustafa III, after an earthquake in 1766 destroyed the original.

4 Eyüp Sultan Mosque (Eyüp Camii)

Also rebuilt after the 1766 earthquake, this mosque *(p82)* at the top of the Golden Horn is one of the holiest places in Islam. It is built around the tomb of a 7th-century saint, Eyüp el-Ensari, standard-bearer of the Prophet Mohammed.

5 Atik Valide Mosque (Atik Valide Camii)

One of Istanbul's finest mosques *(p104)* and Sinan's last great work, the "Old Mosque of the Sultan's Mother" was built on Üsküdar's highest hill. It was completed in 1583 for the formidable Nurbanu, wife of Selim III and mother of Murat III.

6 Church of St George (Ortodoks Patrikhanesi)

The Church of St George *(p84)* stands within the Greek Orthodox Patriarchate complex. Built in 1720, it includes a superb 11th-century mosaic of the Virgin Mary.

7 Church of St Mary of the Mongols (Kanlı Kilise)

Princess Maria, illegitimate daughter of Byzantine Emperor Michael VIII Palaeologos, married Khan Abaqa of the Mongols. On his death in 1282, she founded a convent and this church *(p84)* – Istanbul's only Greek Orthodox church to have been granted immunity from conversion to a mosque by Mehmet II.

**Towering minarets of the
Süleymaniye Mosque Complex**

8 Christ Church

Consecrated in 1868 as the Crimean Memorial Church, this fine Gothic Revival building *(p90)* was renovated and renamed in the 1990s. It is the largest Protestant church in Istanbul.

9 Church of St Anthony of Padua (Sent Antuan)

The Church of St Anthony of Padua *(p90)* is Istanbul's largest Roman Catholic church. Built in 1906–12, it is home to a small community of Franciscan monks.

10 Armenian Patriarchate (Ermeni Patrikhanesi)

🅿 E6 🏠 Sevgi Soh 6, Kumhapı

The Armenians came in numbers to Istanbul in 1461, invited by Sultan Mehmet II to help rebuild the city after its capture in 1453. Opposite the patriarchate building, the Church of the Holy Mother of God (Surp Asdvadzadzin) serves as the main church for the now sadly dwindling Armenian community.

**Chandeliers in the nave of the
Armenian Patriarchate**

TOP 10
TIPS ON
ISLAMIC ETIQUETTE

Women in traditional hijabs

1. Covering the Head
It is essential for women to cover their heads when entering a mosque.

2. Dress
Dress modestly – no bare knees, shoulders or midriffs.

3. Shoes
You must remove your shoes before entering a mosque or a Turkish home.

4. Physical Contact
Avoid physical contact, especially kissing and hugging, while in and around mosques.

5. Sightseeing
Don't go sightseeing in mosques at prayer times (particularly around midday on Fridays).

6. Joking about Islam
Don't joke about Islam or criticize anything related to it.

7. Left Hand
In some Islamic countries one should avoid eating or passing food with the left hand; in Turkey this is not observed.

8. Pork and Alcohol
Although people in Turkey do drink alcohol, you should never offer alcohol or pork to a Muslim – and be considerate when consuming around others.

9. Family Rooms
Some restaurants have separate family rooms *(aile salonu)* into which women will automatically be given entry. Men may only sit there with their families.

10. Ramazan *(Ramadan)*
Be mindful when eating in public during the month of Ramazan.

OFF THE BEATEN TRACK

Neve Shalom synagogue, home to the Jewish Museum

1 Jewish Museum
🏛 F2 📍 Neve Shalom Synagogue, Büyük Hendeh Cad 39, Karahöy
🕐 Hours vary, chech website
🌐 muze500.com 🎟

This interesting little museum is housed in the Neve Shalom synagogue, near the Galata Tower. The museum tells the story of the Jewish people who were offered sanctuary in Istanbul following their expulsion from Spain in the late 15th century.

2 Column of Marcian (Kıztaşı)
🏛 C4 📍 Junction of Kıztaşı Cad with Dolap Sokah, Fatih

Shorter in height but more impressive than the better-known Çemberlitas (Column of Constantine), this granite column dates from the 5th century and has an ornate Corinthian capital with eagles, as well as a plinth carved with Nike, the goddess of victory.

3 Zoodochus Pege (Balıklı Kilise)
🏛 A6 📍 Balıklı Silivrihapı Soh 3, Zeytinburnu 📞 (0212) 582 30 81
🕐 8:30am–4:30pm daily

This beautiful 19th-century Greek Orthodox church is set in lush, green Christian and Muslim cemeteries. In a basement shrine, holy carp swim gracefully in the crystal-clear spring waters.

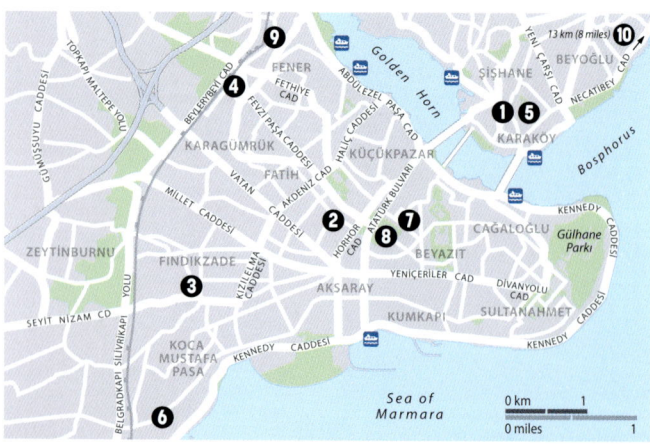

4 Mihrimah Sultan Mosque (Mihrimah Sultan Camii)
B2 **Fevzi Paşa Cad 353, Edirnekapı** **Dawn–dush daily**

A masterpiece created by the Ottoman architect Sinan (p35) and dedicated to the beautiful Mihrimah, daughter of Sultan Süleyman the Magnificent, this delightful mosque stands dramatically atop the Old City's highest hill.

5 Depo
G2 **Lüleli Hendek Cad 12, Beyoğlu** **11am–7pm Tue–Sat** **depoistanbul.net**

Housed in a former tobacco warehouse, this hip but socially conscious gallery has an ever-changing series of exhibitions. Many of the shows focus on more offbeat subjects, such as the plight of Turkey's Christian minorities, political protests and the like. There are also regular documentary screenings.

6 Safa Meyhanesi
A6 **İlyasbey Cad 169, Yedikule** **(0212) 585 55 94**

Arguably the city's most atmospheric meyhane (tavern), Safa Meyhanesi is located in the historic Yedikule quarter, a short stroll from the fortress of the same name. The decor hasn't changed since the 1940s, with vintage rakı (aniseed spirit) posters adorning the walls, high ceilings and wooden floors. Drink rakı, eat meze and fish and be merry.

7 Vefa Bozacısı
E4 **Vefa Cad 66, Fatih** **8am–midnight daily** **vefa.com.tr**

Even if you don't fancy drinking the fermented millet drink (boza) for which

Corridor in the courtyard of the Mihrimah Sultan Mosque

this charming place is known, it's well worth visiting for the late-19th-century interior, with its cut glass, dark wood and blue-and-white İznik tiles. The boza is made in the back.

8 Istanbul Municipality Building
D4 **15 Temmuz Şehitleri Cad, Fatih** **(0212) 455 13 00**

Built in 1953, this huge, rectangular building's grid-like façade brought international, modern architecture into the heart of the Old City, apposite when you consider that Le Corbusier was influenced by Ottoman architecture following a visit to the city in 1911.

9 Edirnekapı Pigeon Fanciers' Market (Güvercin Pazarı)
C2 **Ayvansaray, Hoca Çakır Cad 70**

Every Saturday and Sunday, pigeon fanciers from across the city come to buy and sell tumbling pigeons at this bazaar in the shadow of the Byzantine Palace of the Porphyrogenitus (p84). Grab a glass of tea in the teahouse opposite and soak up the atmosphere.

10 Emirgan Park
Istanbul's most colourful park (p98) is located near the Bosphorus, just above the second suspension bridge. Dotted with kösks, little wooden pavilions resembling Swiss chalets, it has a small lake and a children's play area. The park is awash with blooms during April's Tulip Festival (p62).

SHOPS AND MARKETS

1 Caferağa Medresesi
Originally created by the famed architect Sinan *(p35)* as a *madrasah* (theological school), this structure *(p70)* is home to a variety of traditional craft shops producing and selling their wares.

2 Çarşamba Street Market (Çarşamba Pazarı)
🅟 C3
So famous is this lively street market that the entire district is named Çarşamba (Wednesday) after the day of the week it is held. Many stalls are stacked with fruit, vegetables, cheeses, spices, dried fruit and nuts. Others concentrate on cheap clothing, while more traditional items include thin wooden rolling pins used to make flat breads and brass coffee grinders. The sprawling market stalls occupy several streets to the north and west of Fatih Mosque, where the area is devoutly Muslim.

3 Grand Bazaar (Kapalı Çarşı)
One of the oldest, biggest and most exciting shopping malls in the world, the Grand Bazaar *(p32)* was set up to trade silk, spices and gold in the 15th century – and still sells all three, alongside jazzy glass lampshades, leather jackets and, of course, highly prized Turkish carpets.

4 İstiklal Caddesi
The city's main modern shopping street, İstiklal Caddesi *(p87)* is packed day and night throughout the week. If you need a break from hunting for bargain designer clothes (in İş Merkezi) or vintage clothes in Syrian Passage (Suriye Pasajı), there are plenty of cafés to choose from.

5 Çukurcuma
Many travellers fall in love with this charming old quarter *(p88)* of Beyoğlu, with its eclectic antiques and second-hand dealers, whose wares flow out onto the streets around Turnacıbaşı Sokağı. It is great for a morning's browsing.

6 Zorlu Centre
🅟 C4 🏠 Koru Sokak, Zincirlikuyu
🆆 zorlucenter.com
Designed by one of Turkey's foremost architecture practices, Tabanlioğlu, this state-of-the-art mall in a suburb

Upscale shopping complex, Zorlu Centre

overlooking the 15th July Martyrs' Bridge is worth seeing. It contains the PSM performance hall, a host of trendy shops and a high-tech cinema, as well as Istanbul Raffles Hotel.

7 Nişantaşı
📍 C5

Nişantaşı and neighbouring Teşvikiye are where local fashionistas spend their money on a variety of international brands, including Versace and Dior.

8 Arasta Bazaar (Arasta Çarşısı)

This small, upmarket bazaar (p70) offers the best souvenir shopping in Sultanahmet. Originally built to provide money for the upkeep of the Blue Mosque, it sells good-quality carpets, jewellery and handicrafts in a relatively calm environment, conveniently close to many major sights and hotels.

9 Bağdat Caddesi, Kadıköy
📍 U4

Nicknamed the "Champs-Élysées of Istanbul", this wide boulevard is lined with upmarket boutiques and international brands.

10 Spice Bazaar (Mısır Çarşısı)

Also known as the Egyptian Bazaar (p76), this is the best place in town to buy little presents, with a sea of spice stalls, piles of Turkish delight and plenty of cheap-and-cheerful souvenirs.

Lanterns and other goods on sale at the Grand Bazaar

TOP 10 THINGS TO BUY

1. Jewellery
Precious metals are sold by weight, with a mark-up for workmanship. There are plenty of options, including designing your own jewellery.

2. Carpets
Carpets are the true glory of Turkish art – and you can have one on your own hall floor.

3. Leather
Jackets, bags, wallets and belts are great value and come in all styles, colours and qualities. Again, have your ideas custom-designed if you have enough time.

4. Clothes
Shop around and you can find good-quality clothes and great design at reasonable prices.

5. Textiles
Both cottons and silks are made here and are reasonably priced. Silk scarves are a great-value present.

6. Spices
Great heaps of coloured spices are hard to resist. If you buy saffron, check it's the real thing – there's a cheaper alternative (safflower) on sale.

7. Historic Reproductions
Reproduction Ottoman miniatures are easy to carry and look great back at home.

8. Souvenirs
Shop for hand-woven towels and items handmade from felt.

9. Blue Beads
The ubiquitous blue bead is actually a charm to ward off the "evil eye"; believe that or not, they make attractive gifts.

10. Food
Turkish delight, almonds and hazelnuts, pomegranate molasses and all sorts of other edibles make great presents.

Traditional spices for sale

LOCAL DISHES

1 Meze

Evening meals in Turkey often begin with *meze* – collections of small starters. The range of *meze* is vast, and you can easily eat enough for a whole meal. Cold options range from *haydari* (yogurt with mint and garlic) to *midye pilaki* (mussels cooked in olive oil) or *çerkez tavuğu* (cold shredded chicken in a bread-thickened walnut sauce). Hot options may include chicken liver kebabs, calamari, grilled cheese, or something more adventurous such as *koç yumurtası* (fried sheep's testicles).

2 Pastries

Delicious sweet pastries are sold in dedicated shops and by street vendors; some restaurants will offer them as dessert. The most famous is baklava (flaky pastry drenched in syrup), but there are plenty of variations, including those with honey, syrups, marzipan, almonds and pistachios. All are heavenly to eat.

3 İmam Bayıldı ("The Imam Fainted")

This strangely named dish of aubergine stuffed with tomatoes and onions is a Turkish classic – the Imam in question supposedly found it so delicious that he passed out in ecstasy. Aubergine is a fundamental ingredient of Turkish cuisine; it is said that Ottoman court chefs could prepare it in 150 ways.

4 Dolma

The word *dolma* means "filled up" and is used to describe any stuffed food, from walnuts to peppers, beef, tomatoes or aubergine. The most common version, eaten cold, is vine leaves stuffed with rice, onion, nuts and herbs.

5 Kebabs and Köfte

Turkey's most famous culinary export is the kebab – called *kebap* in Turkish. *Döner kebap* is wafer-thin slices of roast meat (usually lamb) carved from a spit; the *şiş kebap* is cubed lamb or chicken grilled on a skewer. *Köfte* is

Trays containing different types of syrupy baklava

Traditional Turkish breakfast served with *meze*

minced meat cooked as meatballs or flattened onto a skewer and grilled as an *izgara kebap*.

6 Çoban Salatası ("Shepherd's Salad")

This side salad combines tomato, cucumber, chopped pepper, lettuce, parsley, celery, lemon juice and olive oil in a light, healthy, colourful and refreshing dish. Turkish tomatoes are among the finest in the world.

7 Seafood

Istanbul's proximity to the sea means that *taze balık* (fresh fish) is very popular with locals. The catch of the day is often grilled and served with rice or chips and salad. Shellfish and calamari are served as *meze*. A delicious Black Sea dish is *hamsi pilavı* (fresh anchovies and rice).

8 Stews (Güveç)

Often served in traditional *lokanta* restaurants and generally popular in winter, hearty stews are mostly made with lamb, tomatoes and onions.

9 Börek

These savoury pastries are served either as part of a *meze* tray or on their own as fast food. They can be flat or rolled and are filled with cheese and parsley, spinach or meat. They make an excellent light snack.

10 Mantı

This meat-filled Turkish ravioli is topped with yoghurt sauce and tomato butter and sprinkled with dried mint, oregano, red pepper and sumac. Some restaurants also offer a decadent *kızarmış* (fried) version of this boiled dish or a combo plate split between the two. Occasionally, you will find vegetarian versions stuffed with potatoes, spinach or even aubergine.

TOP 10 ISTANBUL SPECIALITIES

1. Gözleme
A *gözleme* is a large rolled-out pancake with a savoury stuffing.

2. İşkembe Çorbası
Tripe soup is a local delicacy and is said to be very good for hangovers.

3. Kanlıca Yoghurt
Firm and creamy, the yogurt from Kanlıca is the city's finest.

4. Lokum
Turkish delight was invented by an Istanbul sweetmaker (*p91*). It's now available everywhere and in multiple flavours. The original shop in Bahçekapı, at Hamidiye Cad 81, is still open.

5. Simit
A *simit* is a round sesame-studded bread, which is quite similar to a New York pretzel.

6. Maraş dondurması
Maraş dondurması (mastic ice cream) uses wild orchid tubers as a thickening agent. The ice cream is able to stretch into a "rope" 60 cm (2 ft) long.

7. Rakı
A clear spirit, *rakı* is an aniseed-based liquor similar to the Greek *ouzo* and is usually drunk after being diluted with water.

8. Aşure
Also known as Noah's pudding, this celebratory dish is said to have been first made by Mrs Noah, from the scraps remaining on the Ark at the end of the flood.

9. Elma Çayı
You may be offered this apple tea as an alternative to ordinary tea when visiting carpet shops.

10. Çay and kahve
Both *çay* (tea) and *kahve* (coffee) are drunk black, strong and sweet, in small quantities.

Black tea with lemon

NIGHTS OUT

1 Jazz
Legendary jazz musician Dizzy Gillespie visited Istanbul in 1956, and that same year the city's first jazz club, 306, opened in Bebek. Stalwarts on the scene include Nardis *(p92)* and Salon İKSV *(p92)*, which hosts the annual Istanbul Jazz Festival *(caz.iksv.org)*.

2 Whirling Dervish Ceremonies
Founded by Sufi poet Rumi in the 13th century, the whirling dervishes dance as a form of meditation – a way to draw closer to God. *Mevlevis* (performers) wear long black cloaks, symbolizing the weight of their ego, which are cast off during the *sama* (the whirling), to show liberation. Performances last around two hours; established venues include Hodjapasha Cultural Centre *(p78)* and Galata Mevlevi House Museum *(p88)*.

3 Shisha Bars
Nargile, or hookah pipes, were introduced to Turkey – by way of India and Iran – in 1603 by Sultan Ahmet I, and to have one was a symbol of status. Heated gently by coals, the tobacco is often flavoured (popular options are strawberry and apple), and the smoke is softened by passing through water. Karaköy *(p97)* has the largest concentration of shisha bars.

4 Theatre
Touring companies from all over Europe come to perform in Istanbul. English-language performances are usually on offer at Zorlu Centre *(p54)*, Salon İKSV *(p92)* and the theatre inside the Atatürk Cultural Centre *(p92)*.

5 Bosphorus Dinner Cruise
Traverse the Bosphorus Strait on an evening cruise *(p42)* that combines sunset views of the city skyline with dinner and live entertainment such as belly dancing. Tours usually include transfers to and from your hotel.

6 Hammams
Prior to plumbing, these public bathing houses with central marble steam rooms were the only means of keeping clean, and many, such as Çemberlitaş *(p38)*, are marvels of Ottoman architecture. You're never naked; you'll be wrapped in a *peştamal* (towel) and then scrubbed with an exfoliating glove, rinsed and massaged by a same-sex attendant. Most operate different hours for men and women.

7 Belly-dancing show
There's a misconception that during the Ottoman Empire the sultan's concubines performed belly dances to seduce him. In fact, as early

**Ataturk Cultural Centre, a venue
for English-language theatre**

as the 1400s, travelling groups of
dancers called *chengis* were invited to
entertain the female harem. One of the
best performances can be enjoyed at
the Hodjapasha Cultural Centre *(p78)*.

8 Nightclubs
Istanbul attracts world-class DJs.
Taksim Square *(p89)* is the main focal
point for clubs, but elite options, such
as Frankhan *(p92)*, are spread between
the districts of Beşiktaş and Ortaköy.

9 Concerts
The city's clash of European and
Asian influences makes for an exciting
line-up of concerts, from classical to
contemporary. The Zorlu Centre *(p54)*
should be your first port of call, but
also try the Art Deco-inspired 1920s
Süreyya Opera House *(sureyyaoperasi.
kadikoy.bel.tr/en)*, Salon İKSV *(p92)* for
classical concerts, or Dorock XL Kadıköy
(535 363 9349) for live bands.

10 LGBTQ+ scene
Homosexuality is legal in
Istanbul, but be aware that public
displays of affection are still quite
frowned upon – whether you're gay
or straight. LGBTQ+-friendly cafés,
bars and clubs are concentrated
around Beyoğlu, Kadıköy, Kurtuluş
and Beşiktaş. For casual drinks, try
Café Mor Kedi *(0212 244 2592)*, and for
dancing, Tek Yön Club *(tekyon.club)*.

**A belly-dancing show at the
Hodjapasha Cultural Centre**

TOP 10
ROOFTOP BARS

1. 360
Perched atop Mısır Apartment, 360
(p92) serves up live entertainment,
from fire swallowers to violinists.

2. Mikla
Sleek and dimly lit, Mikla *(p93)* is
known for its award-winning food,
but the cocktails are pure class, too.

3. 16 Roof
⊞ H1 ⌂ Swissôtel The Bosphorus
Istanbul, Acısu Sok 19 ⊠ swissotel.
com/hotels/istanbul
Rub shoulders with Istanbul's hip
crowd at this multi-level terrace with
sweeping views. DJs on weekends.

4. Simone
⊞ F2 ⌂ RUZ Hotel, General
Yazgan Sok 6 ⊠ ruzhotels.com
Signature cocktails and 360-degree
views define this boutique bar.

5. Balkon
⊞ F2 ⌂ Şehbender Sok 5
⊠ balkonbeyoglu.com
Sip to a soundtrack at this laid-back bar
with a concise list of classic cocktails.

6. Vogue Restaurant
⊞ U3 ⌂ BJK Plaza, Süleyman Seba
Cad 48 ⊠ voguerestaurant.com
Faultless sushi and uber-sexy
cocktails are the order of the day
at this see-and-be-seen hangout.

7. Seven Hills
⊞ G6 ⌂ Cankurtaran, Tevkifhane
Sok 8 ⊠ sevenhillsrestaurant.com
Seafood restaurant and bar that
delivers the best view of the Blue
Mosque and Ayasofya (Haghia Sophia).

8. The Bank Roof Bar
Upscale option above The Bank hotel
(p117) in the hip Karaköy district.

9. The Roof at the Ritz-Carlton
⊞ H1 ⌂ Süzer Plaza Askerocaği
Cad 6 ⊠ morecravings.com/tr/
venues/the-roof
Expect Ibiza vibes thanks to its
cabanas and knock-your-socks-off
pool, which is clear on one side.

10. Restaurant 24
Sophisticated sips on the top floor
of the George Hotel Galata *(p115)*.

ISTANBUL FOR FREE

1 Mısır Apartment
🅿 F1 📍 İstiklal Cad 163, Beyoğlu
This stylish Art Nouveau apartment block is home to a number of small but well-regarded art galleries, including Zilberman Gallery and Galerı Nev. It's also worth heading up to the chic rooftop bar-restaurant, 360 (p92). Here, you can enjoy a free panorama of Istanbul or treat yourself to a pricey drink.

2 Ottoman Mosques
One of the greatest glories of Istanbul is its stunning array of domed Ottoman-era mosques, each flanked by one or more slender minarets. Many of the mosques have delightful interiors encrusted with pretty İznik tiles; all have that indefinable air of tranquillity.

3 Churches
Many Byzantine churches were turned into mosques during the Ottoman era, but the city retained a substantial Christian community until after World War I. Several churches are still in use and give a glimpse into the lives of a dwindling community. Try the Neo-Gothic Church of St Anthony of Padua (p90) or the Greek Orthodox Church of St George (p84).

4 Gülhane Park Cistern
🅿 S3 📍 Gülhane Park, Fatih
🕙 10am–7pm Tue–Sun
This well-preserved cistern was built between the 5th and 7th centuries.

It was rediscovered in 1913 when part of the former Topkapı Palace grounds (p22) were converted into a public park.

5 Park Life
With a population of at least 17 million, Istanbul can seem an incredibly congested city. Join the locals and escape to one of the city's green and historic parks. The best of these are Emirgan (p98), Gülhane (p70), Yıldız on the Bosphorus and Caddebostan in Kadıköy.

6 Walking the Theodosian Walls
These 5th-century triple defences (p48) saved Constantinople from Attila the Hun and many others for over 1,000 years. They have survived remarkably well, and walking their 6-km (4-mile) length from the Sea of Marmara north to the Golden Horn is a series of fascinating steps back into the past.

7 SALT Beyoğlu
🅿 F1 📍 İstiklal Cad 136, Beyoğlu
🅦 saltonline.org
This non-profitmaking gallery opened in a grand, old 19th-century apartment block on bustling İstiklal Caddesi in 2011 and is now one of the city's premier exhibition spaces. There's

also a bookshop, screening room and rooftop winter garden in the complex.

8 Meşher
📍 F2 🏠 İstiklal Cad 211, Beyoğlu
🌐 mesher.org

Meşher is a beautifully restored example of the European-style apartments that were built in the late 19th century along iconic İstiklal Caddesi, then known as the Grande Rue de Péra. It displays fascinating exhibits, showcasing everything from Byzantine artifacts to contemporary art.

9 Koç Research Centre for Anatolian Civilizations
📍 F2 🏠 Merhez Han, İstiklal Cad 181, Beyoğlu 🌐 anamed.ku.edu.tr

This centre hosts exhibitions on the city's archaeological and cultural history. It is part of Koç University and has a library upstairs, accessible only to researchers.

10 Karaköy Fish Market
📍 F3

Just west of the Galata Bridge in Karaköy is a fish market; look out for the *hamsi* (anchovies) piled up in season. Walk west along the waterfront towards the Haliç metro bridge and admire the ferry-filled waters of the Golden Horn.

Gülhane Park, home to a well-preserved cistern

TOP 10 BUDGET TIPS

A busy street-food stall

1. Street Food
Street vendors sell snacks, such as bagel-like *simits*, rice and chickpeas and *tantuni* (spicy stir-fried meat).

2. Public Transport
The Istanbulkart *(istanbulkart. istanbul)* saves up to 33 per cent per journey on public transport.

3. Entertainment
Numerous street entertainers perform on ferries and in metro stations.

4. Alcohol
Restaurants that serve alcohol with meals are always more expensive.

5. Art Galleries
There are many free art galleries around İstiklal Caddesi, and street art in alternative Kadıköy.

6. Discounts
For discounts on Istanbul's top sights, get a Museum Pass *(muze.gov.tr/ MuseumPass)*.

7. Clothing
For affordable clothes, try Beyoğlu İş Merkezi at İstiklal Cad 187, or Terkoz Çıkmazı, an alley off İstiklal Caddesi.

8. Bazaar
The streets surrounding the historic Spice Bazaar are better value than the market itself.

9. Ferries
Ferries up the Golden Horn or to the Princes' Islands are cheaper and just as enjoyable as the Bosphorus Cruise *(p42)*.

10. Nightlife
At most *meyhaneyi* (taverns), it is more economical to get the all-inclusive deal with unlimited drinks.

FESTIVALS AND EVENTS

1 Tulip Festival
Apr
Turkey's national flower is the tulip (*lale*). The tulip motif appeared on İznik tiles and today can be seen on Turkish Airlines aircraft. Each April millions of bulbs bloom across the city, with a competition to judge the best 100. Roadside verges become a riot of colour, but the flowers are best viewed in parks such as Emirgan and Gülhane.

2 Istanbul Film Festival
Apr ⓦ film.iksv.org
Since its inception in 1982, this festival has screened over 3,000 films from 76 countries. A highlight is the Award for Lifetime Achievement, instituted in 1996 – previous winners include American actor Harvey Keitel and Italian star Sophia Loren. Screenings are held in cinemas in Nişantaşı, Beyoğlu and Kadıköy.

3 Sugar Festival (Ramazan Bayramı)
Three days in Apr, dates vary
The Sugar Festival marks the end of the month of Ramazan. People hand out sweets, visit relatives and enjoy cultural events – and Istanbul's bars and clubs are packed with customers again. Many locals take advantage of the holiday period and head out of the city for a few days to escape the hustle and bustle.

4 Conquest of Istanbul
May/Jun
Enjoy recreations of the siege of 1453, performances by the Ottoman Mehter military band, fireworks and much more during the Conquest celebrations. Festivities last a week, but the major spectacle usually takes place on 29 May.

5 Istanbul Music Festival
Jun ⓦ muzik.iksv.org
An impressive array of talented soloists, various ensembles and world-famous orchestras has graced the stages of this prestigious music festival since it was established in 1973.

6 Istanbul Jazz Festival
Jun/Jul ⓦ caz.iksv.org/en
The Jazz Festival was established as an independent event in 1994. The musical range is broad, and you are as likely to encounter Björk or Elvis Costello as you are Brad Mehldau. The choice of venues is eclectic, with traditional clubs, outdoor stages and even a boat on the Bosphorus.

Jacob Collier performing at the Istanbul Jazz Festival

Colourful flower displays
at the Tulip Festival

7 Feast of Sacrifice (Kurban Bayramı)

Four days in Jun/Jul, dates vary
Also known as Eid-ul-Adha, the Feast of
Sacrifice commemorates the Qur'anic
version of Abraham's sacrifice. It falls
two months and ten days after the
end of Ramazan (Ramadan). Muslims
traditionally celebrate the day by slaugh-
tering a sheep on the first morning of
the festival. Friends and family are
invited to a lavish meal, but much of the
meat goes to charity. Note that this is
Turkey's major annual public holiday –
nearly everything closes, and public
transport is seriously limited.

8 Istanbul Biennial

**Sep–Nov, every other year
(odd numbered years) ☑ bienal.
iksv.org**
Istanbul's Biennial showcases
contemporary visual arts from Turkey
and around the globe. Each festival
is directed by a curator of a different
nationality, who chooses a theme and
arranges the programme of exhibitions,
conferences and workshops. Since 2017,
a work of art created for the festival is
gifted to the city following the Biennial.

9 Istanbul International Puppet Festival

**Oct–Nov ☑ istanbulkuklafesti
vali.com**
Karagöz, or Turkish Shadow Theatre,
is a form of traditional Ottoman entertainment suitable for the whole family.
Puppeteers come from as far as China
to showcase their creations.

10 Istanbul Marathon

Nov ☑ maraton.istanbul
Every November, athletes have the
chance to take part in the world's only
transcontinental marathon. The 15th
July Martyrs' Bridge closes for part
of the day to allow those taking part
to cross from Europe to Asia. Register
online in advance to participate.

TOP 10 NATIONAL HOLIDAYS

1. New Year's Day
Istanbul rings in the new year with
fireworks over the Bosphorus.

2. National Sovereignty and Children's Day
The nation celebrates the formation
of the Turkish parliament and
Children's Day on 23 April.

3. International Workers' Day
A day for workers to call for their
rights, 1 May is sometimes marred
by violence as police crack down
on protests.

4. Commemoration of Atatürk
The celebration of Atatürk's birthday
coincides with the Youth and Sports
Day on 19 May. School children mark
the day by marching through the
streets of Turkey.

5. Navy Day
Turkey's strong maritime forces are
honoured on 1 July.

6. Democracy and National Unity Day
Declared a holiday in 2016, 15 July
marks the failed coup by a part of
the Turkish Armed Forces.

7. Armed Forces Day
Turkey's military, the second largest
armed force in NATO, is celebrated
each year on 26 August.

8. Victory Day
Turkey's victory over invading
Greek forces in 1922 is celebrated
on 30 August. The main celebration
is held in Ankara, where the president
leads officials in laying wreaths and
then delivers the keynote address to
commemorate the day.

9. Republic Day
On 29 October, the public celebrates
Atatürk's establishment of the Turkish
republic in 1923, with fireworks, concerts and cultural events.

10. Commemoration of the Death of Atatürk
One minute's silence is observed each
year at 9:05am on 10 November in
memory of Mustafa Kemal Atatürk
(p41), who died on this day in 1938.

AREA BY AREA

Istanbul's Grand Bazaar

KAPALIÇARŞI
GRAND BAZAAR

Satılan malların renkliliği
ve çeşitliliğini öne
çıkaran yalın bir mimari
anlayışı benimsemişti.
Kubbe ve kemerlerdeki
süslemeler 1894
restorasyonunda
eklenmiştir.

YapıKredi

SULTANAHMET AND THE OLD CITY

Many of the city's greatest sights are to be found in this historic area. Recorded history here begins around 667 BCE, when Greek king Byzas founded Byzantium on Seraglio Point (now home to the Topkapı Palace). After his arrival in 324 CE, Constantine transformed this port into the dazzling jewel of Constantinople, a new capital for the Roman Empire. Once the Ottomans seized power in 1453, they too stamped their authority – both religious and secular – on its buildings.

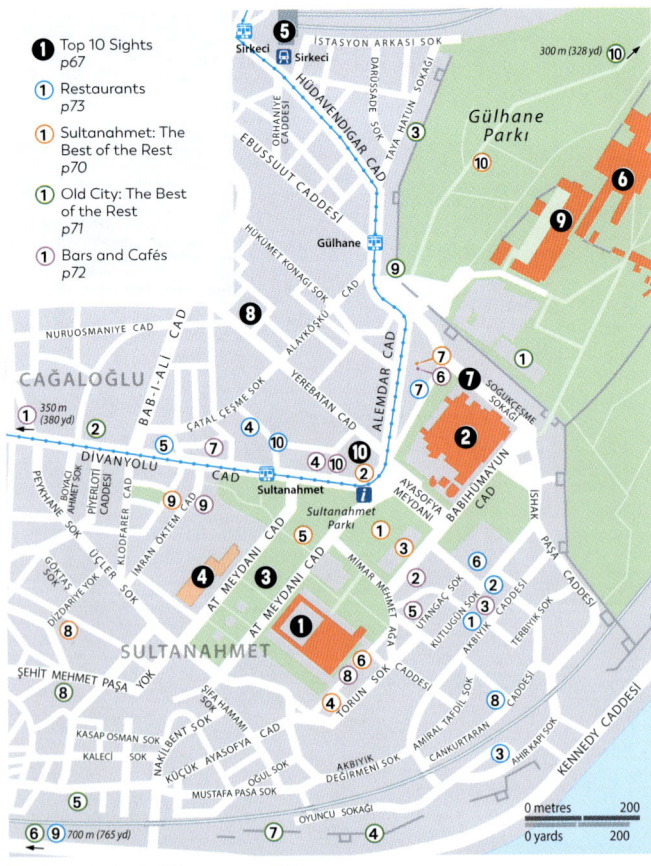

① Top 10 Sights
p67

① Restaurants
p73

① Sultanahmet: The Best of the Rest
p70

① Old City: The Best of the Rest
p71

① Bars and Cafés
p72

For places to stay in this area, see p114

1 Blue Mosque (Sultanahmet Camii)

Begun in 1609, Sultan Ahmet I's mosque (p28) was built opposite Ayasofya and over Constantine's Great Palace to stress the supremacy of Islam and the Ottoman Empire over Christian Byzantium.

Six slender minarets of the iconic Blue Mosque

2 Ayasofya (Haghia Sophia)

Built in 537, this magnificent monument (p26) has withstood wars and earth-quakes. The scale of its vast central dome was not surpassed until the construction of St Peter's in Rome a millennium later. Initially consecrated by Emperor Justinian as the "Church of Holy Wisdom", it was turned into a mosque in 1453 after the fall of Constantinople to the Ottomans, then a museum in 1935 under Atatürk's secular revolution. In 2020, President Recep Tayyip Erdoğan declared it a practising mosque once more.

3 Hippodrome (At Meydanı)
🅿 Q5

Now a park, the Hippodrome was once a Byzantine chariot racetrack – a stadium capable of holding 100,000 people. Laid out in the 3rd century CE by Emperor Septimius Severus, it was enlarged and connected to the adjacent Great Palace by Constantine. There are three great monuments in the Hippodrome: the Egyptian Obelisk (c 1500 BCE) – also known as the Obelisk of Theodosius (Dikilitaş) – which Theodosius transported from Luxor; the Serpentine Column (Yılanlı Sütun) from the Temple of Apollo at Delphi in Greece, made in 479 BCE; and the Column of Constantine VII Porphyrogenitus (Örmetaş), which is of unknown date and was named after the emperor who had it restored in the 10th century. The stadium once held four bronze horses, but these were looted by the Crusaders in 1204 and are now in St Mark's Basilica in Venice.

4 Museum of Turkish and Islamic Arts (Türk ve İslam Eserleri Müzesi)
🅿 Q5 🏠 Meydanı Cad 12 🕐 9am–9pm daily 🌐 muze.gov.tr 🗘

This museum is housed in the vast palace built by İbrahim Paşa (c 1493–1536), Grand Vizier to Süleyman the Magnificent. It contains a collection of more than 40,000 artifacts dating from the 7th century to the present, with exhibits of fine art, crafts and Turkish domestic life in its evolution from nomad's tent to modern home. There's also an exquisite collection of Seljuk and Ottoman rugs, including a priceless 13th-century masterpiece.

Terracotta jar, Museum of Turkish and Islamic Arts

Stained-glass window with intricate design, Sirkeci Station

5 Sirkeci Station (Sirkeci Garı)

R2 Ankara Cad (0212) 520 65 75 Museum: 9am–12:30pm & 1–5pm Tue–Sat

Opened in 1890, the glamorous eastern terminus for the *Orient Express* service was built by German architect August Jasmund in an eclectic style drawing together elements of Istanbul's varied architectural traditions. The station also houses a railway museum and a restaurant. Since the opening of the Marmaray line in 2013, this grand old station is no longer the terminus for trains from Europe, but a mere stop on the metro – albeit the last one before the continent-linking Bosphorus Tunnel.

6 Topkapı Palace (Topkapı Sarayı)

The great palace *(p22)* of the Ottoman Empire was both the residence and the centre of government of the early sultans. The whole complex can take a full day to explore; highlights include the Harem and the Treasury.

7 Soğukçeşme Sokağı

R4

This steeply cobbled street, which runs between the outer walls of the Topkapı Palace and Ayasofya, is a sequence of pretty Ottoman merchants' homes. The street was restored as part of a 1980s project that was one of the first of its kind in Istanbul. Nine of the houses have been incorporated into the Hagia Sofia Mansions hotel, which is part of the Hilton chain.

8 Cağaloğlu Hammam (Cağaloğlu Hamamı)

Q3 Prof Kazım İsmail Gürhan Cad 34 9am–10pm Mon–Thu, 9am–11pm Fri–Sun cagalogluhamami.com.tr

One of the city's best-known and most picturesque bathhouses, the Cağaloğlu Hamamı was built in 1741 by Sultan Mahmut I to raise funds to support his library in Ayasofya. International and historical figures, from King Edward VIII and Florence Nightingale to Cameron Diaz and Harrison Ford, are all reputed to have bathed here. Over the years, the hammam has also been used as a location for countless films and fashion shoots.

9 Archaeological Museum (Arkeoloji Müzesi)

This is one of the world's greatest historical museums *(p30)*. It has three principal sections: the Museum of the Ancient Orient, which contains, among other things, the city gates of Babylon; the Tiled Kiosk, with a superb display of ceramics; and the main museum, where royal sarcophagi discovered by archaeologist Osman Hamdi Bey at Sidon in Lebanon are the star exhibits.

Admiring sculptures at the Archaeological Museum

SÜLEYMAN I

Süleyman I, "the Magnificent", ruled over the Ottomans for 46 years. During that time, he doubled the size of the Empire and, as caliph (supreme head of the Islamic faith), consolidated Sunni authority over Shia Islam. A great patron of the arts, he also compiled the Codex Süleymanicus, which defined the concept of justice and guaranteed equal treatment for all.

10 Basilica Cistern (Yerebatan Sarnıcı)

📍 R4 🏛 Yerebatan Cad 1/3 🕐 9am–11:50pm daily 🌐 yerebatan.com ♿

Known as the "Sunken Palace" in Turkish, the Basilica Cistern was built as a vast underground water-storage tank. Built on the site of an old Roman basilica (hence the name), the cistern was begun by Constantine and, in 532, expanded by Justinian to ensure that Constantinople was always supplied with water. Covering around 9,800 sq m (105,000 sq ft), it once held about 80 million litres (18 million gallons). The cistern roof is supported by 336 pillars, 8 m (26 ft) high. Look for the upside-down Medusa heads, reused from older buildings. This unusual tourist attraction is also popular as a film location and a venue for concerts.

A DAY IN SULTANAHMET

Morning

Start your day at the dawn call of the *müezzin*, and visit the **Blue Mosque** (*p28*) after the prayer ends. From there, cross the square to **Ayasofya** (*p26*), then pay a visit to the **Basilica Cistern**, the **Hippodrome** (*p67*) and the **Museum of Turkish and Islamic Arts** (*p67*) before strolling through the **Arasta Bazaar** (*p70*) to the **Mosaic Museum** (*p70*). The distance between each of these attractions is small, and most of the sites are fairly simple, so you should be able to visit them all in a single morning. You'll need a little time to relax after this, so choose one of the cafés or restaurants on **Divanyolu Caddesi** (*p70*) for lunch.

Afternoon

Now choose one of two options: either walk across to the **Topkapı Palace** and spend the whole afternoon embroiled in Ottoman court intrigue, or wander through the side streets to the **Cağaloğlu Hammam** for a Turkish bath before rejoining **Soğukçeşme Sokağı** and making your way to the vast **Archaeological Museum** (*p30*). Then, continue down the hill for a stroll along the waterfront at **Eminönü** (*p77*). Take the tram back up the hill to Sultanahmet and choose one of the many rooftop bars or restaurants from which to watch the sun set over the city and the floodlights playing on Ayasofya and the Blue Mosque.

Sultanahmet: The Best of the Rest

**Gazebo-style Kaiser
Wilhelm Fountain**

1. Sultanahmet Square (Sultanahmet Meydanı)
📍 R4

Once the hippodrome that stood at the heart of Constantinople, this square lies between Ayasofya (p26) and the Blue Mosque (p28).

2. The Milion Monument (Milyon Taşı)
📍 R4 🏛 Ayasofya

The marble pilaster of the Milion can be found in the northwestern corner of Sultanahmet Square. From the 4th century CE, it was used as "point zero" to measure distances to the many cities of the Byzantine Empire.

3. Hürrem Sultan Hammam (Hürrem Sultan Hamamı)
📍 R5 🏛 Ayasofya Meydanı
🕐 8am–10pm daily 🌐 hurrem sultanhamami.com

These opulent baths were built for Süleyman the Magnificent in 1556 and are named after the sultan's powerful and influential wife.

4. Great Palace Mosaic Museum (Büyük Saray Mozaikleri Müzesi)
📍 R5 🏛 Arasta Bazaar 📞 (0212) 518 12 05 🕐 For renovation 📱

Little remains of Emperor Justinian's vast 6th-century palace except for an elaborate mosaic floor.

5. Kaiser Wilhelm Fountain
📍 R5 🏛 At Meydanı

German Emperor Wilhelm II gifted this Neo-Byzantine fountain to Sultan Abdül Hamit II in 1901.

6. Arasta Bazaar (Arasta Çarşısı)
📍 R5 🏛 Mimar Mehmet Ağa Cad 2 🕐 9am–9pm daily

The bazaar was originally built to provide revenue for the Blue Mosque. Today, there are around 40 shops selling carpets, textiles, jewellery and other souvenirs.

7. Caferağa Medresesi
📍 R4 🏛 Caferiye Sok, Soğukkuyu Çıkmazı 5 📞 (0212) 513 36 01 🕐 9am–6pm Tue–Sun

Watch craftspeople create art, from ceramics to calligraphy, in this 16th-century Qur'anic college, then take the product home or sign up for a course.

8. Divanyolu Caddesi
📍 Q4

Divanyolu was once the Mese – the main thoroughfare – of Byzantine Constantinople and Ottoman Istanbul, and it continued all the way to the Albanian coast.

9. Cistern of 1,001 Columns (Binbirdirek Sarnıcı)
📍 Q4 🏛 Binbirdirek, İmran Öktem Cad 2 🕐 9am–5pm Mon–Sat 🌐 binbirdirek.com.tr 📱

There are only 224 columns in this 4th-century cistern. It houses several cafés and hosts live music and events.

10. Gülhane Park (Gülhane Parkı)
📍 S3 🏛 Kennedy Cad, Fatih

Translated as "house of roses", this park backs onto Topkapı Palace (p22). It's especially vibrant in spring, when technicolour tulips look almost fake in their uniformity.

Old City: The Best of the Rest

1. Haghia Eirene (Aya İrini Kilisesi)
⊙ S4 **⌂** Topkapı Palace (1st courtyard) **⊙** 9am–5:30pm Wed–Mon ⏵
Built in the 6th century on the site of an earlier church, Haghia Eirene was the city's cathedral until the construction of Ayasofya (p26). It is now home to a museum and hosts concerts.

2. Imperial Tombs
⊙ F5 **⌂** Divanyolu Cad
Designed by Garabet Balyan, the tombs of three of the last Ottoman sultans, Mahmut II, Abdül Aziz and Abdül Hamid II, lie beside busy Divanyolu in a peaceful graveyard.

3. Museum of the History of Science and Technology in Islam
⊙ R2 **⌂** Gülhane Park **⊙** 9am–7pm daily **⊠** muze.gov.tr ⏵
Among the exhibits at this well-organized museum are fantastic models of scientific inventions.

4. Sea Walls
⊙ P1–S1 **⌂** Kennedy Cad
Believed to be built by Septimius Severus and extended by Theodosius II (p49), the walls are best viewed from the main coastal road.

5. Church of SS Sergius and Bacchus (Küçük Ayasofya Camii)
⊙ F6 **⌂** Küçük Ayasofya Camii Sok **⊙** Dawn–dusk daily ⏱ Prayer times
Known as "Little Haghia Sophia", this church was built in 527 and converted into a mosque in 1500. The marble columns and carved frieze with a Greek inscription are all original.

6. Kumkapı
⊙ E6
The old Byzantine harbour of Kumkapı is now home to many fish restaurants.

7. Bucoleon Palace
⊙ F6 **⌂** Kennedy Cad
Three vast marble windows stare sightlessly out to sea from this last standing fragment of the Great Palace, built into the sea wall.

8. Sokollu Mehmet Paşa Mosque
⊙ P5 **⌂** Şehit Mehmetpaşa Yhş **⊙** Dawn–dusk daily ⏱ Prayer times
Built by Sinan for Grand Vizier Sokollu Mehmet Paşa, this mosque contains some fine İznik tiles, an elaborately painted ceiling and four tiny black stones from the Kaaba in Mecca.

9. Alay Pavilion (Alay Köşkü)
⊙ R3 **⌂** Topkapı Palace
Built into the outer walls of the Topkapı Palace (p22), this small imperial pavilion overlooked the Sublime Porte, the entrance to the seat of government in later Ottoman times. Sultan İbrahim took pot shots at passers-by from here.

10. Column of the Goths
⊙ S2 **⌂** Gülhane Park
Erected to commemorate a great Roman victory over the Goths in the 3rd century, this fine 18-m- (60-ft-) high column is topped by an ornate Corinthian capital.

İznik tiles in Sokollu Mehmet Paşa Mosque

Patrons at the Çorlulu Ali Paşa Medresesi

Bars and Cafés

1. Çorlulu Ali Paşa Medresesi
N4 Yeniçeriler Cad 38
Lounge on cushions in one of several atmospheric teashops with locals puffing on *nargile* (bubble pipe). No alcohol.

2. Istanbul Kahvehanesi
R5 Cankurtaran, Kabasakal Cad 5
This quiet little courtyard café, close to the Blue Mosque, serves fantastic homemade cookies.

3. Just Bar
R5 Akbıyık Cad 28, Fatih
(0538) 914 29 39
A friendly, boisterous spot, Just Bar serves tasty cocktails and beers on one of the main Sultanahmet hotel strips. Expect a party vibe.

4. Lale Restaurant Pudding Shop
Q4 Divanyolu Cad 6 puddingshop.com
Once an essential stop on the "Hippy Trail", with a message board and copious quantities of cheap food, Lale is great for visitors. The food is good value, the service is friendly and they offer draught beer and free Wi-Fi.

5. North Art Coffee
R5 Utangaç Sok 21
Brunch is served with a Turkish twist at this café. If you're looking for a delicious latte (complete with latte art), this is the place to come.

6. Çaferağa Medresesi
R4 Caferiye Sok
Enjoy a cup of coffee or opt for a light meal in the courtyard of this atmospheric, Sinan-designed *medrese*, near Ayasofya (Haghia Sophia).

7. Çiğdem Pastanesi
Q4 Divanyolu Cad 56 cigdempastanesi.com
Enjoy traditional Turkish tea or a well-made cappuccino at this classic patisserie. For a light snack, try the sticky, honey-drenched baklava.

8. Café Meşale
R5 Arasta Bazaar
A quiet place for a cup of tea and *nargile* during the day, in the evening Café Meşale becomes a restaurant with live music and traditional whirling dervish performances.

9. Istanbul Terrace Bar
Q4 Arcadia Blue Hotel, Dr Imran Oktem Cad 1
This bar offers superb views of the Old City, Bosphorus, Sea of Marmara and hills of Asia.

10. Hafız Mustafa 1864 Edebiyat Kıraathanesi
R4 Divan Yolu Cad 14
This branch of a long-standing Turkish sweet seller offers a staggering variety of traditional Turkish cakes and desserts, as well as great coffees and teas.

Restaurants

1. Albura Kathisma
R5 **Akbıyık Cad 38**
(0533) 430 24 97 · ₺₺
One of the best restaurants on Akbıyık Caddesi, this spot serves a good mix of Ottoman, Turkish and international dishes in atmospheric surroundings. It also has some delicious vegetarian options.

2. Palatium Café and Restaurant
S5 **Kutlugün Sok 33, Fatih** **palatiumcafeandrestaurant. com · ₺₺**
Dine on hearty kebabs, soft flatbreads and casseroles in a relaxed, cheerful setting. Alcohol is served, too.

3. Giritli
R5 **Keresteci Hakkı Sok 8**
(0212) 458 22 70 · ₺₺₺
Fine fish and a bountiful array of unusual *meze* are the stars at this Cretan-style restaurant.

4. Khorasani
Q4 **Ticarethane Sok 9/B** **khorasanikebab.com · ₺₺₺**
Khorasani's traditional southeast-Turkish specialities are delicious. The emphasis is on freshly prepared kebabs cooked over charcoal.

Diners enjoying a meal in a *meyhane* in Kumkapı

5. Amedros
Q4 **Hoca Rüstem Sok 3, off Divanyolu** **amedroscafe.com · ₺₺**
This bistro serves Turkish and European food, with good vegetarian options.

6. Avlu
R5 **Four Seasons Hotel, Tevfikhane Sok 1** **(0552) 402 31 00 · ₺₺₺**
Located in the Four Seasons Hotel, Avlu serves modern Anatolian cuisine. Enjoy a meal on its terrace garden.

7. Matbah
R4 **Ottoman Hotel Imperial, Caferiye Sok 6** **matbahrestaurant.com · ₺₺₺**
Tasty Ottoman and Turkish classics are served in a lovely terrace restaurant.

8. Balıkçı Sabahattin
R5 **Seyit Hasankuyu Sok 1, off Cankurtaran Cad** **balikcisabahattin.com · ₺₺₺**
Established in 1927, this is one of the city's finest fish restaurants.

9. Kumkapı
M5 · ₺₺
There are many *meyhanes* (taverns) in this old fishing neighbourhood, serving fish and *meze* with *rakı*. Musicians play *fasıl* and expect to be tipped.

10. Mozaik Restaurant
Q4 **İncirli Çavuş Sok 1, off Divanyolu** **(0537) 683 64 97 · ₺₺**
This restaurant, set in a restored 19th-century Ottoman house, serves Turkish and international favourites.

BAZAAR QUARTER AND EMINÖNÜ

In 1453, after his conquest of Constantinople, Sultan Mehmet II chose this area, close to the Graeco-Roman Forum of the Bulls, as the place to begin construction of a model city based on Islamic principles. The key elements were mosques and *medreses* (religious schools), charitable institutions, accommodation for travellers and a Grand Bazaar – the latter funding all the others and a great deal more besides. All these were constructed – and many still remain – in one of the city's most fascinating and vibrant districts, where you can buy, with equal ease, a plastic bucket and an antique silk carpet, an ancient religious text or a kilo of peppercorns.

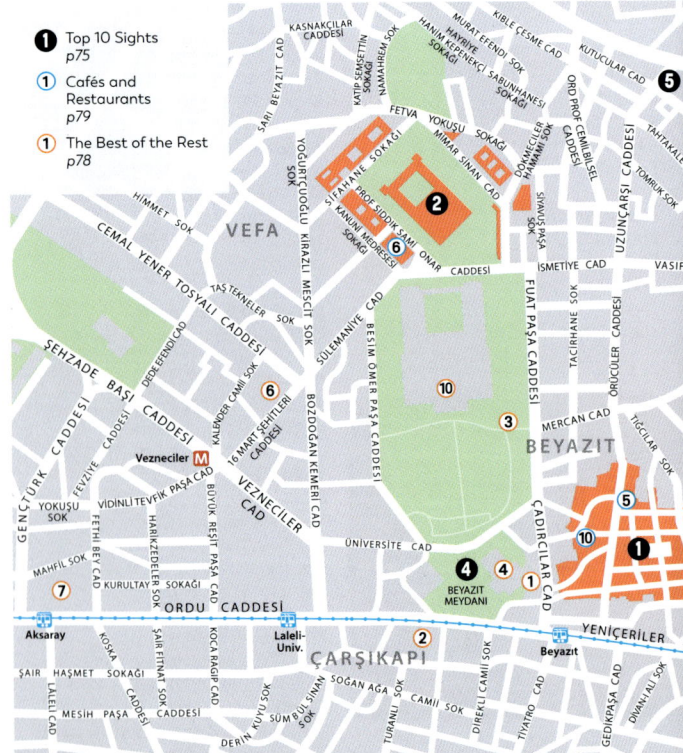

1️⃣ Top 10 Sights
p75

1️⃣ Cafés and Restaurants
p79

1️⃣ The Best of the Rest
p78

For places to stay in this area, see p114

Richly decorated interior of the Süleymaniye Mosque

1 Grand Bazaar (Kapalı Çarşı)

The bazaar (p32) was one of the first institutions established by Mehmet II shortly after his conquest of the city. Its oldest part is the domed İç Bedesten, a lockable warehouse used for trading and storing the most valuable wares. Today, along with covered streets containing thousands of shops and stalls, there are cafés, restaurants and teahouses. Several *hans* – originally travellers' inns – are now mostly workshops and small factories.

2 Süleymaniye Mosque Complex (Süleymaniye Camii)

Built for Süleyman I in 1550–57, this is the largest and most lavish mosque in the city (p34). Süleyman and his wife Hürrem Sultan are both buried here, while Mimar Sinan, the architect of the mosque, is buried just outside the main complex in a tomb he designed and built himself.

3 Çemberlitaş Hammam (Çemberlitaş Hamamı)

Nurbanu, wife of Selim II (son of Süleyman I and Hürrem Sultan), commissioned these baths (p38) from Sinan in 1584. Their gracious domed halls make them a popular tourist attraction.

4 Beyazıt Square (Beyazıt Meydanı)

🗺 M3

This grand open space has been one of the city's principal meeting places for centuries. Popularly known as Beyazıt Square, its official name is Freedom Square (Hürriyet Meydanı). It stands on the site of the late Roman Forum Tauri (Forum of the Bulls), which was extended by Emperor Theodosius in 393. The forum gained its name from the bronze bull at its centre, a place of sacrifice in the pre-Christian era. Some of its colonnades were reused in the building of the Basilica Cistern (p69), while others lie abandoned along the tram tracks on Ordu Caddesi. The square is home to the Beyazıt Mosque and Istanbul University.

Detail on an İznik tile, Rüstem Paşa Mosque

5 Rüstem Paşa Mosque (Rüstem Paşa Camii)
 N1 ⚐ Mahkeme Sok ☎ (0212) 526 73 50 ⏰ 9am–dusk daily

This enchanting mosque was built in 1561 by Sinan. It was commissioned by Süleyman the Magnificent's daughter Mihrimah in memory of her husband, Rüstem Paşa, Süleyman's Grand Vizier. The mosque blazes with richly coloured İznik tiles, inside and out, while galleries and windows flood the hall with light.

6 Column of Constantine (Çemberlitaş)
⚐ P4 ⚐ Divanyolu Cad

Built of Egyptian porphyry, this column, 35 m (115 ft) tall and topped by a statue of Emperor Constantine dressed as Apollo, once stood in the centre of the Forum of Constantine. It was erected in 330 to celebrate the inauguration of the Roman Empire's new capital. Constantine buried holy

Galata Bridge spanning the Golden Horn

relics – said to have included the axe Noah used to build his ark – around the base. Its Turkish name, Çemberlitaş (Hooped Column), refers to the reinforcing metal hoops added in 416 and replaced in the 1970s.

7 Spice Bazaar (Mısır Çarşısı)
⚐ P1 ⚐ Eminönü ⏰ 8am–7:30pm daily

This marketplace was built in 1660 as part of the New Mosque complex. Its Turkish name, meaning Egyptian Bazaar, derives from the fact that it was originally financed by duties on Egyptian imports, although it is better known in English as the Spice Bazaar because, for centuries, spices were the main goods sold here. These days, the bazaar has turned into a major tourist attraction. The bazaar, and the streets around it, are the best places to buy small presents, from *lokum* (Turkish delight) and phials of saffron, to pistachios, almonds, incense and coffee.

8 Galata Bridge (Galata Köprüsü)
⚐ F3

The predecessor of this modern bridge across the Golden Horn was an iron pontoon structure built between 1909 and 1912. It was underequipped for modern traffic and was replaced in 1994 by the current two-level concrete bridge. The city views from the lower level, especially at sunset, are breathtaking. Parts of the old bridge, further up the Golden Horn near Ayvansaray, have been rebuilt.

9 Eminönü
🗺 N1

From the Grand Bazaar, steep alleys crowded with market stalls lead down to the Eminönü waterfront. It's a great place to roam, with mosques and markets, a bank of ferry piers and street sellers offering everything from *simits* (*p57*) to fake watches.

10 New Mosque (Yeni Camii)
🗺 P1 📍 Eminönü 📞 (0212) 512 23 20 🕐 9am–dush daily

This large, rather gloomy mosque was commissioned in 1597 by Valide Sultan Safiye, mother of Sultan Mehmet III. Work was interrupted when the architect was executed for heresy and Safiye was banished after her son's death. It was finally completed in 1663. The interior is richly decorated but has relatively poor-quality İznik tiles.

EMPEROR CONSTANTINE

The son of an army officer, Constantine (c 272–337) became sole emperor of the Roman Empire in 324 and soon declared Christianity the state religion. In 325, he called the Council of Nicaea, which laid down the basic tenets of the faith. In 330, he inaugurated his new capital, Constantinople. He formally converted to Christianity on his deathbed.

A DAY'S SHOPPING

Morning

Start the day refreshed after a visit to the **Çemberlitaş Baths** (*p38*), then pop into the **Nuruosmaniye Mosque** (*p78*) before heading to the **Grand Bazaar** (*p32*). Take a break at one of the cafés in the bazaar and enjoy a coffee, then walk on through **Beyazıt Square** (*p75*) and down the hill to **Süleymaniye Mosque** (*p34*) to see the tombs of Süleyman and Hürrem Sultan. A good option for lunch is the casual **Özen Lokanta** (*Süleymaniye, Mimar Sinan Cad 3*).

Afternoon

Head further along İsmetiye Caddesi, then turn left into Uzunçarşı Caddesi and head down the hill through crowded market streets, where metal- and woodworkers still ply their trade, before turning right on **Tahtakale Caddesi**, a sensory treat with its traditional spice and coffee sellers. Carry on downhill to Eminönü, where you can visit the **Rüstem Paşa Mosque** and look at the **New Mosque** before a last round of shopping in the **Spice Bazaar**. Between the New Mosque and the Spice Bazaar is the market for flowers, plants, seeds and songbirds. Have dinner at **Hamdi Et Lokantası** (*p79*) or **Ocak** (*p79*) near Sirkeci Station (*p69*) or take the tram back up to Sultanahmet and choose a rooftop bar or restaurant from which to enjoy sunset views.

The Best of the Rest

Intricate carvings inside the Nuruosmaniye Mosque

1. Second-Hand Book Bazaar (Sahaflar Çarşısı)
🗺 M4 ⬚ Medrese Çık, behind the Beyazıt Mosque ⬚ Dawn–dush daily (some shops closed on Sun)

Manuscripts have been traded here since medieval times, although printed books were banned until 1729. Now, mostly academic textbooks and coffee-table books on Turkey are sold here.

2. Arch of Theodosius
🗺 M4 ⬚ Beyazıt Meydanı

A jumble of massive, fallen columns is all that remains of the 4th-century triumphal Arch of Theodosius. The similarly carved columns in the Basilica Cistern (p69) were clearly taken from here.

3. Beyazıt Tower (Beyazıt Kulesi)
🗺 M3 ⬚ Off Fuat Paşa Cad
⬚ To the public

This elegant marble tower, built in 1828 as a fire lookout, stands in the Istanbul University grounds.

4. Beyazıt Mosque (Beyazıt Camii)
🗺 M4 ⬚ Ordu Cad 📞 (0212) 212 09 22 ⬚ Dawn–dush daily

Built in 1506 for the Ottoman Sultan Beyazıt II, this is the oldest surviving imperial mosque in Istanbul.

5. Atik Ali Paşa Mosque (Atik Ali Paşa Camii)
🗺 P4 ⬚ Yeniçeriler Cad ⬚ Dawn–dush daily

This 15th-century copy of the original Fatih Mosque is named after its builder, who was Grand Vizier to Beyazıt II.

6. Kalenderhane Mosque (Kalenderhane Camii)
🗺 E5 ⬚ 16 Mart Şehitleri Cad
⬚ Dawn–dush daily ⬚ Prayer times

Built on the site of a 5th-century bathhouse, Kalenderhane Mosque was remodelled in the 12th century as the Church of Theotokus Kyriotissa and was later turned into a mosque. Don't miss the superb prayer hall.

7. Laleli Mosque (Laleli Camii)
🗺 D5 ⬚ Ordu Cad ⬚ Prayer times only

The Laleli Mosque was built by Mustafa III in 1763, with lavish use of coloured marble in the new Ottoman Baroque style. Mustafa is buried here.

8. Nuruosmaniye Mosque (Nuruosmaniye Camii)
🗺 P4 ⬚ Vezirhanı Cad ⬚ Dawn–dush daily

Completed by Sultan Osman III in 1755, Nuruosmaniye was the first Ottoman Baroque mosque in the city. The mosque is part of a larger complex that includes an Islamic school and a library.

9. Hodjapasha Cultural Centre
🗺 Q2 ⬚ Hoca Paşa Hamam Sok 3, Sirheci ⬚ For performances only, chech website 🌐 hodjapasha.com

This restored bathhouse forms a superb setting for whirling dervishes.

10. Istanbul University
🗺 M2–3 ⬚ Beyazıt Meydanı
📞 (0212) 440 00 00

Turkey's oldest higher education institution, the university moved to its present campus in 1866. The campus and its grounds are closed to the public.

Cafés and Restaurants

PRICE CATEGORIES

For a typical meal of *meze* and main
course for one without alcohol,
including taxes and extra charges.

₺ under ₺500 ₺₺ ₺500–1,000
₺₺₺ over ₺1,000

1. Pandeli
📍 P1 🏠 Mısır Çarşısı 1 🌐 pandeli.
com.tr · ₺₺₺
Set in a domed, İznik-tiled dining room
above the Spice Market, Pandeli has
been an Istanbul institution since it
opened in 1901. Book in advance.

2. Sirkeci Lokantası 1912
📍 P2 🏠 Cronton Design Hotel,
Hobyar, Rahvancı Sok 5 ☎ (0212)
556 47 20 · ₺₺
Come lunchtime, this ornate café offers
a huge buffet. Coffee and sweet treats
are served all day.

3. Hocapaşa Pidecisi
📍 Q2 🏠 Hoca Paşa Sok ☎ (0212) 512
09 90 · ₺
This humble little spot has been baking
delicious *pide* (flat breads) in a wood-
fired oven since 1964. Order an *ayran*
(yoghurt drink) alongside.

4. Ocak
📍 Q2 🏠 Mimar Vedat Sok, Fatih
🌐 ocak.ist · ₺₺₺
The Reggio Ottoman hotel-restaurant
serves light and flavoursome Turkish-
Anatolian dishes as set menus, including vegetarian options.

5. Şark Kahvesi
📍 N3 🏠 Yağlıkçılar Cad 134 ☎ (0532)
490 20 93 · ₺
Located inside the Grand Bazaar (*p32*),
this lovely café is a popular spot for
tea and coffee.

6. Tarihi Süleymaniyeli Kurufasulyeci
📍 M2 🏠 Süleymaniye, Prof Siddik
Sami Onar Cad 11 ☎ (0212) 513 62 19 · ₺
This restaurant has been serving
simple Ottoman cuisine for 80 years.

7. Kahve Dünyası
📍 P4 🏠 Nuruosmaniye Cad 79
☎ (0212) 527 32 82 · ₺
This is a branch of the popular Turkish
coffeehouse chain.

8. Hamdi Et Lokantası
📍 P1 🏠 Kalçın Sok 11, Eminönü
🌐 hamdi.com.tr · ₺₺₺
Specialities served here include
patlıcan kebabs (minced meat grilled
with aubergine slabs).

9. Lokanta 1741
📍 Q3 🏠 Profesör Kazım İsmail Gürkan
Cad 34, Fatih ☎ (0533) 145 17 41 · ₺₺₺
Set inside the Cağaloğlu Hammam, this
romantic, fine-dining restaurant has a
great wine list and innovative cocktails.

10. Havuzlu Restaurant
📍 N3 🏠 Gani Çelebi Sok 3, Kapalı Çarşı
🕐 D, Sun 🌐 havuzlurestaurant.com · ₺
This place offers excellent kebabs and
meze. Arrive early, as the restaurant can
get crowded.

**Havuzlu Restaurant,
inside the Grand Bazaar**

THE GOLDEN HORN, FATIH AND FENER

The Golden Horn, a fjord-like river inlet that divides the old and new cities of European Istanbul, is enjoying a new lease of life. Often overlooked by visitors, this part of Istanbul is dotted with historic attractions, including Kariye Mosque, the equal of anything on the Historic Peninsula itself. Conservative Fatih has plenty of atmospheric places to eat, while Fener is now a prime real-estate location and the popular setting for television programmes. The Old City shoreline has miles of narrow parks and walkways and the new city shore is home to attractions such as Miniatürk and the Rahmi Koç Museum.

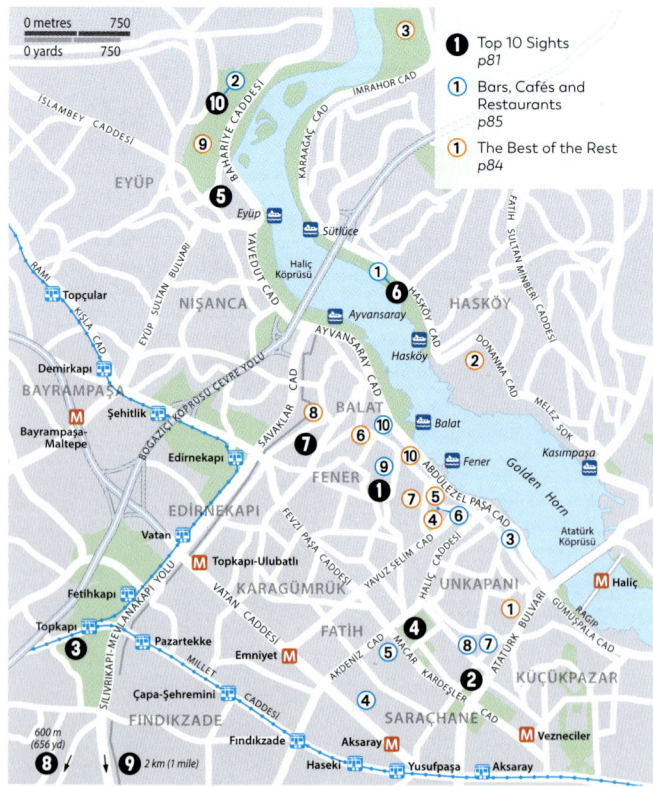

1 Top 10 Sights
p81

1 Bars, Cafés and Restaurants
p85

1 The Best of the Rest
p84

For places to stay in this area, see p115

Mosaic of a Byzantine monk, Fethiye Mosque

1 Fethiye Mosque (Fethiye Camii)

C2 | Fethiye Kapısı Sok | 9am–5pm daily

Built by Emperor John II Comnenus in the 12th century, this was the headquarters of the Greek Orthodox Patriarchate from 1456 to 1568. It was later converted into a mosque, and in 1573 renamed *Fethiye* (Victory) to celebrate Murat III's conquest of present-day Georgia and Azerbaijan. The side-chapel is a museum, containing some of the finest Byzantine mosaics in Istanbul. The church is under restoration and may be closed.

2 Aqueduct of Valens (Bozdoğan Kemeri)

D4 | Atatürk Bulvarı (north side of Saraçhane Parkı)

West of Süleymaniye are the remains of the two-storey aqueduct built by Emperor Valens in 368. Repaired many times in the intervening years, the aqueduct remained in use until the 19th century, bringing water from the Belgrade Forest to the centre of the Great Palace complex.

3 Panorama 1453

A5 | Topkapı Kültür Parkı, Topkapı | 8am-6:30pm daily | panoramikmuze.com

Situated right by the Theodosian Walls (*p48*), this history museum vividly recreates the moment in 1453 when the walls were finally breached. Painted on the inside of a large dome are some 10,000 life-like figures replaying the desperate Byzantine defence against the besieging Ottoman Turks. Take a seat in the museum's helicopter simulator for a bird's-eye view of Istanbul or a historical tour around the country.

4 Fatih Mosque (Fatih Camii)

C3–4 | Fevzi Paşa Cad | 9am–dusk daily

This huge Baroque mosque is the third building to have occupied this site. The first was the Church of the Holy Apostles (burial place of many Byzantine emperors). Mehmet II then constructed Istanbul's first purpose-built imperial mosque here, but it was destroyed in an earthquake in 1766. Today's mosque was built mainly in the 18th century by Sultan Mustafa III. The grounds contain the tombs of Mehmet II and his wife Gülbahar Hatun. There is a colourful market in the surrounding streets on Wednesdays.

Aqueduct of Valens spanning a busy road

5 Eyüp Sultan Mosque (Eyüp Sultan Camii)

📍 B5 🕌 Eyüp Meydanı (off Camii Kebir Cad) 📞 (0212) 564 73 68 🕐 Tomb: 9:30am–4:30pm daily

Istanbul's holiest mosque was built by Mehmet II in 1458, over the *türbe* (burial site) of Eyüp el-Ensari, Prophet Mohammed's friend and standard-bearer who fell during the Arab siege of Constantinople in the 7th century. Eyüp's tomb opposite is one of the holiest pilgrimage sites in Islam (after Mecca and Jerusalem). The mosque courtyard has intricately painted İznik tiles and is usually filled with worshippers queuing to pay their respects.

6 Rahmi Koç Museum (Rahmi Koç Müzesi)

📍 B5 🕌 Hasköy Cad 5 🕐 9:30am–5pm Tue–Fri, 10am–7pm Sat & Sun 🌐 rmk-museum.org.tr ✱

This eclectic museum is named after its founder, the industrialist Rahmi Koç. The main part of the collection, which includes an assortment of vintage cars, is situated in a 19th-century shipyard building. Outside are aircraft, boats, restored shops and a submarine. Across

Vintage car at Rahmi Koç Museum

Grand Eyüp Sultan Mosque, overlooking the Golden Horn

the road, in a restored Ottoman anchor foundry with Byzantine foundations, are model engines, trains, cars and more boats. There is also an excellent café and the gourmet Halat Restaurant.

7 Kariye Mosque (Kariye Camii)

First a church, then a mosque, next a museum, then a mosque again, Kariye Mosque *(p36)* was rebuilt in the late 11th century and restored in the early 14th by Theodore Metochites. He also commissioned the superb series of mosaics and frescoes that he hoped would secure him "a glorious memory among posterity till the end of the world".

8 Zoodochus Pege (Balıklı Kilise)

📍 A6 🕌 Balıklı Silivrikapı Sok 3, Zeytinburnu 🕐 8:30am–4:30pm daily

Surrounded by Christian and Muslim cemeteries, this Greek Orthodox church was built in 1833 on the site of an older church. It is famous for its *ayazma*, or sacred spring, which is full of fish and located beneath the church.

9 Yedikule Fortress (Yedikule Hisarı)

📍 A6 🕌 Yedikule Meydanı Sok 🕐 9am–5pm Tue–Sun 🌐 yedikule hisari.com

This seven-tower Ottoman fortress is built onto a section of the Theodosian

BUILT TO LAST

There were ten fortified gates and 192 towers in the Theodosian Walls. The outer wall is 2 m (6 ft) thick and 8.5 m (28 ft) tall, separated from the 5-m- (16-ft-) thick, 12-m- (39-ft-) high inner wall by a 20-m (66-ft) moat. The walls of Byzantium were built to withstand anything, and did so for 1,000 years. They were finally breached in 1453.

Walls (p48). Built within its outer walls is the Golden Gate, a triumphal arch that formed the entrance to medieval Byzantium, constructed by Emperor Theodosius I in 390. Concerts and other events are periodically hosted in the castle yard.

10 Pierre Loti

During his time in Istanbul, Pierre Loti – the pseudonym and nom de plume of French sailor, author and Turkophile Julien Viaud – frequented a café in Eyüp, and the surrounding area is now named after him. Arriving in the city in 1876, Viaud fell in love with a local woman whose name he gave to the title of his novel, *Aziyadé*, which chronicles their difficult relationship. The area known as Pierre Loti Hill can be visited via the cable car beside Sultan Eyüp Mosque. The hilltop Pierre Loti Café (p85) affords splendid views of the Golden Horn.

Turkish coffee-making equipment at the Pierre Loti Café

A DAY ALONG THE CITY WALLS

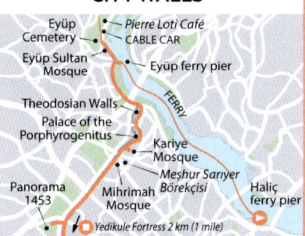

Morning

Take the **Haliç ferry** from Karaköy near the Galata Bridge to Eyüp, then ride the cable car up the tree-clad cemetery hill. Enjoy tea at **Pierre Loti Café** (p85) before heading down through **Eyüp Cemetery** to queue at the **Eyüp Sultan Mosque**. Stroll down the Golden Horn to join the line of the **Theodosian Walls** (p48). Turn south and walk alongside the mighty walls as they march uphill to the **Palace of the Porphyrogenitus** (p84). Deviate slightly from the line of the walls to visit the Byzantine **Kariye Mosque**, with its superb mosaics and frescoes.

Afternoon

Continue south along the line of the walls. The first highlight en route is the **Mihrimah Mosque**, on the Old City's highest hill. Right next to the mosque is **Meşhur Sarıyer Börekçişi** (meshursariyerborekcisi.com), where you can feast on lamb *köfte* and cheese-filled *börek*. About halfway along the length of the walls is **Panorama 1453** (p81), with its recreation of the famous siege of 1453. Continue downhill to **Yedikule Fortress**, a massive Ottoman-era fortress incorporating part of the Theodosian walls and the legendary Golden Gate. Ride the metro back to the centre from the Kazlıçeşme stop.

The Best of the Rest

1. Church of the Pantocrator (Molla Zeyrek Camii)
📍 D3 🏛 Badethane Soh, Küçükpazar ☎ (0212) 532 50 23 🕐 20 mins before and after prayer times

This 12th-century Byzantine church was converted into a mosque in 1453.

2. Aynalıkavak Palace (Aynalıkavak Kasrı)
📍 D1 🏛 Aynalıkavak Cad, Hasköy 🕐 9am–5:30pm Tue–Sun 🌐 milli saraylar.gov.tr 🔗

This 17th-century Ottoman palace has an interesting exhibition of Turkish musical instruments.

3. Miniatürk
📍 B5 🏛 İmrahor Cad 7, Sütlüce 🕐 9am–7pm daily 🌐 miniaturk.com.tr 🔗

This intriguing park contains 1:25 scale models of 139 of Turkey's most impressive structures, including the Ayasofya and Dolmabahçe Palace. There's also a small maze park here.

4. Yavuz Selim Mosque (Yavuz Selim Camii)
📍 D2 🏛 Yavuz Selim Cad, Fatih 🕐 Tomb: 9am–5pm daily

This elegant 16th-century mosque was built to honour Selim I. His tomb is in the garden.

5. Church of St George (Ortodoks Patrickhanesi)
📍 D2 🏛 Dr Sadık Ahmet Cad 19, Fatih ☎ (0212) 531 96 70 🕐 8:30am–4:30pm daily

This church is the spiritual centre of the Orthodox Church community worldwide.

6. Balat
📍 C2

Balat was once home to the city's Sephardic Jewish community. It houses the Ahrida Synagogue *(0212) 244 19 80)*, one of the oldest in Istanbul. Call ahead to book your visit.

7. Church of St Mary of the Mongols (Kanlı Kilise)
📍 C2 🏛 Firketeci Soh 1, Fener ☎ (0212) 521 71 39

This church was built by a Byzantine princess, Maria Palaiologina, who married a Mongol khan and later became a nun. Knock on the compound door for entry.

8. Palace of the Porphyrogenitus (Tekfur Sarayı)
📍 B1 🏛 Şişhane Cad, Edirnekapı 🕐 10am–6pm Tue–Sun 🌐 tekfur sarayi.istanbul

An annexe of the Blachernae Palace, this is one of the city's best-preserved Byzantine palaces.

9. Eyüp Cemetery
📍 B5 🏛 Cami Kebir Soh

A steep walk leads past hundreds of Ottoman-era gravestones. There's a superb view of the Golden Horn.

10. Church of St Stephen of the Bulgars (Bulgar Kilisesi)
📍 C2 🏛 Mürsel Paşa Cad 85, Balat 🕐 9am–5pm daily

This late 19th-century church was prefabricated in Vienna, in cast iron.

Scale model of the Galata Tower at Miniatürk

Bars, Cafés and Restaurants

Delicious Middle Eastern vegetarian *meze* platter

PRICE CATEGORIES

For a typical meal of *meze* and main course for one without alcohol, including taxes and extra charges.

₺ under ₺500 ₺₺ ₺500–1,000
₺₺₺ over ₺1,000–1,500

1. Café du Levant, Sütlüce
D1 🛒 Kumbarahane Cad 2
☎ (0212) 369 66 16 🕐 Jul–Oct · ₺₺
This café, located just across the road from the Rahmi Koç museum *(p82)*, serves Gallic cuisine.

2. Pierre Loti Café, Eyüp
B5 🛒 Gümüşsuyu Karyağdı Sok 5
☎ (0212) 497 13 13 · ₺
The interior of this hilltop café has traditional tiles, tea-making paraphernalia and exhibits relating to the novelist Pierre Loti. Outside, the terrace offers fine views of the Golden Horn.

3. Cibalikapı Balıkçısı, Fener
E3 🛒 Kadir Has Cad 5 ☎ (0532) 163 55 20 · ₺₺
This traditional tavern serves fresh fish of the day and a wonderful selection of hot and cold *meze*. Lively and informal with good views of the Golden Horn.

4. Akdeniz Hatay Sofrası, Fatih
B5 🛒 Ahmediye Cad 44/A, Aksaray
🌐 akdenizhataysofrasi.com.tr · ₺₺
Choose from a vast array of *meze*, tender kebabs and specialities at this spot known for its for southeast Turkish food.

5. Vezir Han Şark Sofrası
C4 🛒 Ocaklı Sok 9, Fatih
☎ (0532) 209 61 38 · ₺₺
Dine on delicious hummus, baba ghanoush, tabbouleh, kibbeh and other Syrian specialities in a casual, cosy setting in a part of Istanbul that's home to many immigrant communities.

6. Forno Balat
C2 🛒 Fener Kireçhane Sok 13/A
🌐 fornobalat.com · ₺
Sample *lahmacun*, a thin and crispy flatbread topped with spiced ground meat, parsley and a squeeze of lemon, in this bright and contemporary café.

7. Şehzade Cağ Kebap, Fatih
Q2 🛒 Hoca Paşa Sok 6
☎ (0212) 533 33 61 · ₺
Simple place serving *cağ kebapı* from eastern Turkey, marinated lamb slowly roasted on a horizontal spit.

8. Siirt Şeref Büryan, Fatih
D4 🛒 Ömer Efendi Cad, Serdab Sok 34 ☎ (0212) 525 35 81 · ₺₺
This traditional restaurant specializes in *perde pilavi*, a delicious pilau rice cooked in pastry, and *büryan*, lamb slow-cooked in a clay pit. No alcohol is served here.

9. Smelt and Co.
C2 🛒 Kiremit Cad 16, Balat
☎ (0538) 286 54 65 · ₺₺₺
Enjoy an eclectic dining experience in a character-filled, traditional Balat house. Reservations are essential.

10. Balat Sahil Restoran
C1 🛒 Mürselpaşa Cad 245 ☎ (0212) 525 61 85 · ₺₺
This is a good-value tavern where visitors can enjoy the aniseed spirit *rakı* alongside *meze* and fresh fish.

BEYOĞLU

Set on a steep hill north of the Golden Horn, facing the old town of Stamboul, is the "new town" of Beyoğlu, previously known as Pera – simply, "the other side". The area is hardly "new", though; there has been a settlement here for nearly 2,000 years. Populated by Jewish and Genoese merchants in the Byzantine era, Pera became the commercial centre of Istanbul after European embassies were established here in Ottoman times. Today, Beyoğlu is the heart of modern European Istanbul, its streets (such as İstiklal Caddesi) lined with consulates, churches, stylish bars and the latest shops.

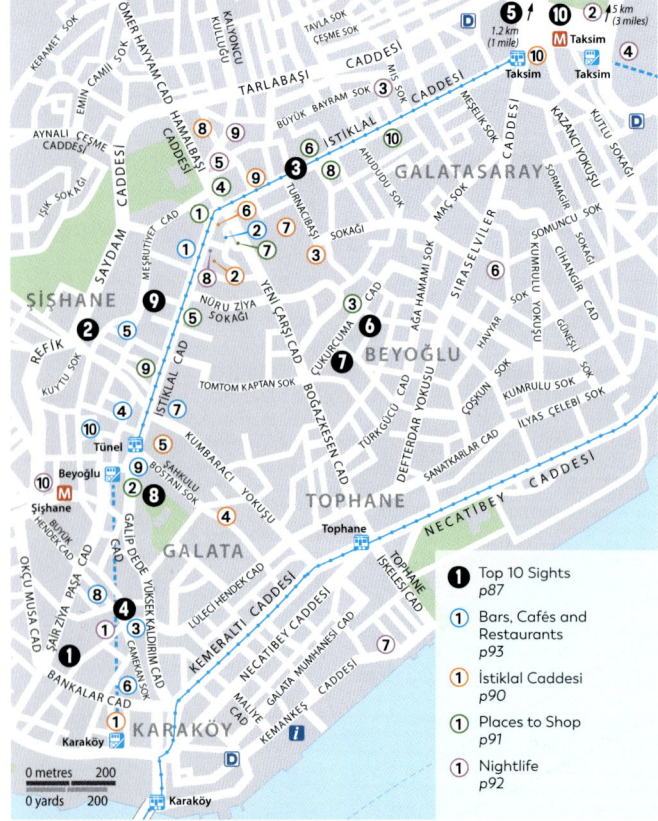

- 1 Top 10 Sights
  p87
- 1 Bars, Cafés and Restaurants
  p93
- 1 İstiklal Caddesi
  p90
- 1 Places to Shop
  p91
- 1 Nightlife
  p92

For places to stay in this area, see p115

1 Church of SS Peter and Paul (Sen Piyer Kilisesi)

📍 F3 🏛 Galata Kulesi Sok 44, Karaköy ⏰ 2:30–5:30pm Fri & Sat 🌐 senpiyer.org/hilise

The Dominican brothers of Galata moved to this site, just below the Galata Tower, after their original church was requisitioned as a mosque in the 16th century. The church was built in the style of a basilica with four side-altars. It also has a blue cupola studded with gold stars over the choir. Mass is said here in Italian every morning. Ring the bell by the tiny door (accessed through the courtyard) to gain admittance.

2 Pera Palace Hotel (Pera Palas Oteli)

Opened in 1892 mainly for travellers arriving on the *Orient Express*, the Pera Palace (*p115*) is Istanbul's most famous hotel. British thriller writer Agatha Christie stayed here often between 1924 and 1933 and is said to have written *Murder on the Orient Express* in Room 411. The hotel has also been frequented by well-known figures such as Mata Hari, Leon Trotsky, Greta Garbo and Atatürk, the "Father of the Turks" (*p41*). In 1981, the Atatürk Museum was opened in the leader's favourite room in the hotel, No. 101. It displays many of his personal items.

Tram trundling along busy İstiklal Caddesi

3 İstiklal Caddesi

📍 F2–G1

Packed with shoppers by day, Beyoğlu's main street is also an entertainment hub by night and home to several interesting sights. It is pedestrianized, but you can hop on the tram, which runs the street's entire length. Be aware that many protests and demonstrations take place here. Visitors are advised to stay well away from them.

4 Galata Tower (Galata Kulesi)

📍 F2 🏛 Büyük Hendek Sok ⏰ 8:30am–11pm daily (last adm: 10pm) 🌐 galatakulesi.gov.tr ↗

One of the city's most distinctive sights, this 67-m- (220-ft-) high tower was built in 1348 by the Genoese, the Byzantine Empire's greatest trading partners, as part of their fortification of Galata. Since then, the tower has survived several earthquakes and been restored many times. A lift climbs 11 floors to the top where there is a balcony with fabulous views of the Golden Horn and the city. Inside the tower, Istanbul's history is chronicled in a small museum.

Elegant interior of the Pera Palace Hotel

5 Military Museum (Askeri Müze)

B5 Vali Konağı Cad, Harbiye 9am–4:30pm Tue–Sun; askerimuze.msb.gov.tr

Housed in the military academy where Atatürk was educated, this museum documents the history of warfare from Ottoman times to World War II. Chain mail, armour, swords and embroidered tents are among the exhibits. A highlight is the show by the Mehter Band (performances 3pm daily), recreating the military music of the Janissaries, the elite Ottoman corps.

6 Çukurcuma

G2

The old quarter of Beyoğlu is today a centre for second-hand and antiques stores. Its restored warehouses and mansions house shops that sell anything from antique cabinets to modern upholstery materials and 1960s comics.

7 Museum of Innocence (Masumıyet Müzesi)

G2 Dalgıç Cıkhmaz 2, Çuhurcuma 10am–6pm Tue–Sun masumiyet muzesi.org

Nobel-prize-winning Turkish author Orhan Pamuk's book *The Museum of Innocence* is the inspiration for this museum. The thousands of cigarette butts that the angst-ridden protagonist of the novel smoked are on display, along with other ephemera, in a converted period town house.

8 Mevlevi Monastery (Mevlevi Tekkesi)

F2 Galip Dede Cad 15 (0212) 245 41 41 9am–7pm Tue–Sun

This late 18th-century lodge belonged to a Sufi sect of Islamic mystics and is now the Whirling Dervish Museum (Mevlevihane Müzesi). Sufi whirling dervishes still dance here on Sundays; look out for times on a board outside and call ahead to book. The museum houses artifacts associated with dervish rituals, such as begging bowls and musical instruments, but the star of the show is the beautiful *semahane*, or ritual dance hall, upstairs.

Osman Hamdi Bey's *The Tortoise Trainer*, Pera Museum

9 Pera Museum (Pera Müzesi)

📍 F2 🏠 Meşrutiyet Cad 65 📞 (0212) 334 99 00 🕐 10am–7pm Tue–Sat (to 10pm Fri), noon–6pm Sun 🌐 peramuseum.org ↗

The old Bristol Hotel has been revived as the home of this museum and gallery, privately run by the Suna and İnan Kiraç Foundation set up by wealthy Turkish industrialists. The first floor displays the Kiraç family's collections of Kütahya tiles and ceramics and Anatolian weights and measures. The next floor has an intriguing collection, most of it by European artists, detailing life at the Ottoman imperial court from the 17th century onwards. The top storeys are given over to temporary shows.

10 Taksim Square (Taksim Meydanı)

📍 G1

Lined by historical landmarks as well as swanky restaurants, bars and hotels, buzzy Taksim Square is the commercial and cultural hub of modern Beyoğlu. It is situated at the end of the water supply line laid down by Mahmut I in 1732 – his original stone reservoir still stands at the square's western end. On the same side of the square is the Monument of Independence, a patriotic sculpture erected in 1928 of Atatürk and other revolutionary heroes.

Whirling dervishes performing at the Mevlevi Monastery

A DAY IN BEYOĞLU

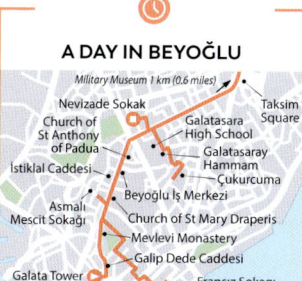

Military Museum 1 km (0.6 miles)

Nevizade Sokak
Church of St Anthony of Padua
İstiklal Caddesi
Galatasaray High School
Taksim Square
Galatasaray Hammam
Çukurcuma
Beyoğlu İş Merkezi
Asmalı Mescit Sokağı
Church of St Mary Draperis
Mevlevi Monastery
Galip Dede Caddesi
Galata Tower
Fransız Sokağı

Morning

Walk over the Galata Bridge and head up to the **Galata Tower** (*p87*). Take the lift to the top to walk the perimeter balcony and enjoy the superb view. Back at the bottom, refresh yourself at a traditional tea garden before taking a stroll up **Galip Dede Caddesi** (*p91*) to peer into the music shops and have a go on a traditional Turkish instrument if the fancy takes you. Continue on towards Tünel (*p90*) and learn about whirling dervishes at the **Mevlevi Monastery**. For lunch, try a small street café on **Asmalı Mescit Sokağı**, or go Gallic at **Fransız Sokağı** (French Street).

Afternoon

Walk up **İstiklal Caddesi** (*p87*) browsing the music shops, fashion stores and **Beyoğlu İş Merkezi** (*p91*), then visit the **Church of St Mary Draperis** and the **Church of Saint Anthony of Padua** (*p90*). Get to the **Military Museum** in time for the 3pm performance by the Mehter Band. Head to **Çukurcuma** via **Taksim Square**, stopping off for some refreshments if you need to. After browsing the antique shops here, relax at the **Galatasaray Hammam** (*p90*). Refreshed, wander past the **Galatasaray High School** (*p90*) and cut through to boisterous **Nevizade Sokak** to choose a place to wine and dine.

İstiklal Caddesi

1. Tünel
🔂 F2

The 573-m (1,880-ft) Tünel is a funicular that runs up the steep slope from Galata Bridge to İstiklal Caddesi. Built by a French engineer in 1874, it is one of the world's oldest metros.

2. Church of St Anthony of Padua (Sent Antuan)
🔂 F1 **🏛** İstiklal Cad 171 **📞** (0212) 244 09 35 **🕐** 8am–7:30pm daily **🕐** 12:30–3pm Sun

This red-brick Neo-Gothic building is the city's largest working Catholic church. The church was built by Istanbul-born Italian architect Giulio Mongeri in 1911.

3. Galatasaray Hammam (Tarihi Galatasaray Hamamı)
🔂 G1 **🏛** Turnacıbaşı Sok 8 (off İstiklal Cad) **🕐** 9am–9pm daily **🌐** galata sarayhamami.com **🔗**

Wealthy Istanbulites come here to be sweated, scrubbed and scraped in one of the finest hammams in Istanbul, built by Beyazıt II in 1481. Today, the baths are fully modernized but still retain their charm. Men and women bathe separately.

Impressive entrance to the Galatasaray High School

4. Christ Church
🔂 F2 **🏛** Serdar Ehrem Sok 52 **📞** (0212) 251 56 16

The centre of Istanbul's Anglican community, this church was consecrated in 1868 as the Crimean Memorial Church.

5. Swedish Consulate
🔂 F2 **🏛** İstiklal Cad 247 **📞** (0212) 334 06 00 **🕐** For events only

Built in 1757, this magnificent embassy was reconstructed after a fire in 1870.

6. Yapı Kredi Kültür Sanat
🔂 F1 **🏛** İstiklal Cad 285 **📞** (0212) 252 47 00 **🕐** 10am–7pm Mon–Fri, 11am–7pm Sat, noon–7pm Sun

This smart art gallery was set up by one of Turkey's largest banks.

7. Galatasaray High School (Galatasaray Lisesi)
🔂 G1 **🏛** İstiklal Cad 159 **📞** (0212) 249 11 00 **🕐** To the public

Originally founded by Sultan Beyazıt II in 1481 to train imperial pages, this is still Turkey's premier school.

8. Fish Market (Balık Pazarı)
🔂 F1

A fish, fruit and veg market by day, by night the adjacent alleys are filled with cheap and lively restaurants.

9. Flower Arcade (Çiçek Pasajı)
🔂 F1

Housed in the Cité de Pera (1876), one of many Victorian arcades along İstiklal, this former flower market is now an entertaining (if touristy) tavern quarter.

10. Nostalgic Tram
🔂 F2–G1

The horse-drawn tram service that rumbled along İstiklal Caddesi in the 19th century was electrified in 1914. Its bright red carriages have become an icon of Beyoğlu. Buy tickets at either end of the line.

Shopping for ceramics and clothes at Aznavur Pasajı

Places to Shop

1. Aznavur Pasajı
G1 **İstiklal Cad 108**

This nine-storey, Italian-style arcade has been on İstiklal Caddesi since 1883. You can buy a range of goods here, including jewellery, clothes and souvenirs.

2. Galip Dede Caddesi
F2

Hand-made musical instruments, including the traditional *oud*, violins and cymbals, are sold at a string of specialist music shops in this street.

3. Çukurcuma
G2

The streets between Cihangir and Galatasaray form part of the old quarter (*p88*) and are the best spots for antique-hunting.

4. Avrupa Pasajı
F1 **Meşrutiyet Cad 8**

The 22 shops in this old arcade carry a fine selection of jewellery, ceramics and other traditional Turkish crafts. There are also quirkier souvenirs such as old prints and maps.

5. Beyoğlu İş Merkezi
F2 **İstiklal Cad 187**

A haven for bargain-hunters, the three-storey Beyoğlu İş Merkezi is filled with tiny shops selling high-street fashion labels. Many of the products here are second-hand or surplus, hence the rock-bottom prices. A tailor's shop in the basement can make alterations on the same day.

6. Koton
G1 **İstiklal Cad 52, İstiklal Mall** **koton.com**

You'll find both men's and women's fashions at this reasonably priced Turkish chain store. Designs are updated regularly and include party- and daywear.

7. Homer Books
G2 **Yeni Çarşı Cad 52** **homerbooks.com**

One of the best-stocked bookshops in the city, Homer Books has English-language titles on all matters Turkey and Istanbul. Staff here are English-speaking, too.

8. Mavi Jeans
G1 **İstiklal Cad 153** **mavi.com**

Jeans made from organic cotton and hip Istanbul T-shirts are among the stylish items available from one of Turkey's most popular fashion brands.

9. By Retro
F2 **Suriye Pasajı 166/C**

Set at the end of the historic Syria Passage arcade, this store sells vintage clothing and other retro goods.

10. Ali Muhiddin Hacı Bekir
G1 **İstiklal Cad 83A** **haci behir.com**

The place for *lokum* (Turkish delight), this is the Beyoğlu branch of the confectioners who invented the stuff in 1777. Other treats include *akide* (boiled sweets), *helva* and baklava.

Live music at trendy Babylon

Nightlife

1. Nardis Jazz Club
◻ F3 ◻ Kuledibi Sok 8 ◻ Sun
◻ nardisjazz.com
There's live music every night except Sunday. Find a table near the stage and choose from the menu of salads and pasta.

2. Babylon
◻ Bomonti Bira Fabrikası 1, Şişli
◻ babylon.com.tr
Housed in a converted brewery north of Taksim Square, Babylon is indisputably the city's best venue for live music of every kind, especially alternative foreign and Turkish bands.

3. Mektup
◻ F1 ◻ İman Adnan Sok 20, off İstiklal Caddesi ◻ (0212) 249 11 67
One of the best places in Beyoğlu to listen to Turkish folk music and have a glass of beer.

4. Atatürk Cultural Centre
◻ H1 ◻ Mete Cad 2 ◻ akmistanbul. gov.tr
Enchanting opera, orchestra and ballet performances take the main stage at this architecturally striking cultural complex on Taksim Square. Plays and film screenings are also hosted regularly.

5. Kastel Club
◻ F1 ◻ Hüseyinağa, Kamer Hatun Cad 10 ◻ (0533) 215 30 96
Flit between Kastel Club's rooftop terrace and its dance hall, housed in an ornate building complete with ceiling frescoes.

6. Minimuzikhol
◻ G2 ◻ Soğancı Sok 3, off Sıraselviler Cad ◻ minimuzikhol.club
This small, lively club attracts discerning clubbers who come for the techno, dubstep and hip-hop. Internationally acclaimed DJs also perform here on occasion, check the website for shows.

7. Frankhan
◻ G3 ◻ Kemankeş Cad 73, Karaköy
◻ frankhan.istanbul
Both local and international DJs spin records for an energetic crowd until late in this two-part hall located near Galataport and the waterfront.

8. 360
◻ F1 ◻ İstiklal Cad 163
◻ 360istanbul.com
On weekends especially, people flock to this chic rooftop club with superb views. It offers lounge music with dinner, and a resident DJ for a funkier dance sound after midnight.

9. Peyote
◻ F1 ◻ Kameriye Sok 4, off Hamalbaşı Cad ◻ (0212) 251 43 98
This popular local venue for alternative and world-music bands draws a young crowd with its low prices and up-and-coming acts.

10. Salon İKSV
◻ F2 ◻ Sadi Konuralp Cad 5, off Refik Saydam Cad ◻ saloniksv.com
An intimate venue for classical, jazz, world music, plus dance and theatre.

Bars, Cafés and Restaurants

PRICE CATEGORIES
For a typical meal of *meze* and main course for one without alcohol, including taxes and extra charges.
....
₺ under ₺500 ₺₺ ₺500–1,100
₺₺₺ over ₺1,000

1. Mandabatmaz
🗺 F1 🏠 Olivia Geçidi, off İstiklal Cad
🌐 mandabatmaz.com.tr · ₺
Sit on low stools in this hole-in-the-wall café to drink Istanbul's very best, rich and aromatic Turkish coffee at a bargain price.

2. Kafe Ara
🗺 F1 🏠 Ara Güler Sok 2, off Yeni Çarşi Cad 📞 (0212) 245 41 05 · ₺₺
There's an intellectual, artistic vibe at this café serving fresh, light food (but no alcohol). It is decorated with the work of Turkey's most famous photographer, Ara Güler.

3. Otantik Café
🗺 F3 🏠 Camekan Sok 4 📞 (532) 578 50 63 · ₺
A charming café serving Turkish coffee, apple pie and other treats, Otantik is a stone's throw from Galata Tower.

4. Refik'a
🗺 F2 🏠 Sofyali Sok 6–8 📞 (0212) 243 28 34 · ₺₺
A true *meyhane* with *meze*, free-flowing wine and alternative clientele, Refik'a is stuck in the past and all the better for it.

5. Mikla
🗺 F1 🏠 The Marmara Pera, Meşrutiyet Cad 15, Beyoğlu 🌐 mihlarestaurant. com · ₺₺
Anatolian specialities get a modern makeover at this cool rooftop restaurant. The food and views are sublime.

Cosy outdoor seating at Kafe Ara

6. Salon Galata
🗺 F3 🏠 Banhalar Cad 3/A, Karahöy 📞 (0212) 252 7256 · ₺₺
Contemporary Mediterranean fare is served in the old-fashioned, high-ceilinged dining room here.

7. Yeni Lokanta
🗺 J6 🏠 Kumbaracı Yokuşu 66, Beyoğlu 🌐 yenilohanta.com · ₺₺₺
A top-notch restaurant, Yeni Lokanta specializes in traditional Turkish dishes with a contemporary flavour.

8. Sensus
🗺 F2 🏠 Büyüh Hendeh Cad 5, Galata
🌐 sensuswine.com · ₺₺
This trendy basement wine bar stocks dozens of different Turkish wines and a range of cheeses to go with them. Weekend nights are packed, so make sure to arrive early.

9. Hasan Fehmi Özsüt
🗺 F2 🏠 İstiklal Cad 261 🌐 karahoy ozsut.com.tr · ₺
This Beyoğlu institution has been serving traditional Turkish breakfasts since 1915. Their *kaymak*, a rich clotted-cream like item, is made from buffalo milk from their farm in Tekirdağ.

10. Aheste
🗺 F2 🏠 Asmalı Mescit, Meşrutiyet Cad 107 📞 (0212) 243 26 33 🕐 L · ₺₺₺
Aheste is Persian for "slowly" and this cool spot's *meze* dishes are meant to be shared and savoured.

THE BOSPHORUS

The Bosphorus is one of the world's busiest waterways, part of the only shipping lane from the Black Sea to the Mediterranean. Just 32 km (20 miles) long and varying in width from 3.5 km (2.2 miles) to 698 m (2,290 ft), it connects the Black Sea to the Sea of Marmara, dividing Europe from Asia. The straits are governed by international maritime law, so Turkey only has authority over vessels flying a Turkish flag. Navigation can be difficult, since the mixture of fresh water from the Black Sea and salt water from the Sea of Marmara creates strong cross-currents. All of this is fascinating, but, to most visitors, the draw is the beauty of the waterway and the historic buildings that line its shores.

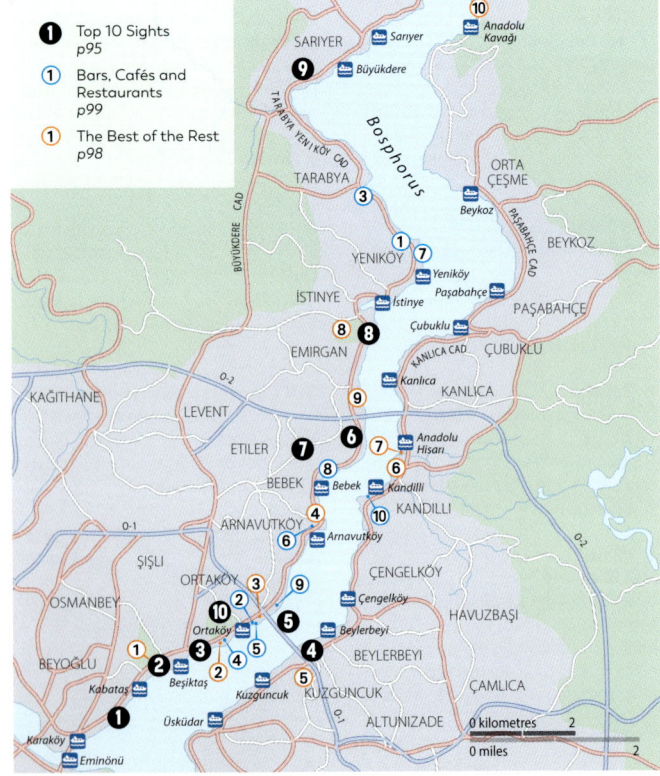

1 Top 10 Sights
p95

1 Bars, Cafés and Restaurants
p99

1 The Best of the Rest
p98

For places to stay in this area, see p116

Maritime-themed exhibits at the Naval Museum

1 İstanbul Modern (İstanbul Modern)

G2 🏠 Kılıç Ali Paşa Mahallesi Tophane İskele Cad 1/1, Beyoğlu 🕐 10am–6pm Tue–Sun (to 8pm Fri) 🌐 istanbulmodern.org 🔗

The fine collection of modern Turkish painting, sculpture and photography at this cutting-edge gallery is augmented by touring exhibitions, video and audio installations, and an arthouse cinema. In addition to the main gallery spaces, the complex includes a large public square, a restaurant, a café, a bookstore, a library and plenty of indoor and outdoor event spaces.

2 Dolmabahçe Palace (Dolmabahçe Sarayı)

In 1856, Sultan Abdül Mecit removed his entire family and government from the Topkapı to this European-style palace *(p40)* on the Bosphorus shore.

3 Naval Museum (Deniz Müzesi)

C5 🏠 Beşiktaş Cad 6, Sinanpaşa 📞 (0212) 327 43 45 🕐 9am–5pm Tue–Fri, 10am–5pm Sat & Sun 🔗

Conveniently located right on the banks of the Bosphorus, this state-of-the-art museum celebrates Ottoman Turkey's great maritime history. Exhibits to look out for, on the main floor, include a few imperial *caïques* – high-prowed barges that were used for ferrying the royal family along the Bosphorus. The largest, built for Sultan Mehmet IV in 1648, was 40 m (130 ft) long and required 144 *kürekçis* (rowers) to steer it. Beautifully carved figureheads, along with a chronological display of the Ottoman naval history, are housed on the floor below.

4 Beylerbeyi Palace (Beylerbeyi Sarayı)

C5 🏠 Abdullahağa Cad (next to 15th July Martyrs' Bridge) 🕐 Apr–Sep: 9am–5pm Tue–Sun; Oct–Mar: 9am–4pm Tue–Sun 🌐 millisaraylar.gov.tr 🔗🔗

This small, frivolously ornate powder-puff of a palace was built between 1860 and 1865 by Sultan Abdül Aziz as a summer retreat. It was here that Sultan Abdül Hamit II *(p97)* lived out his days in captivity after he was deposed in 1909. You will either be charmed or overwhelmed by the incredible detailing of architect Sarkis Balyan's Rococo-Gothic style. Look for the striking inlaid stairs in the Fountain Room, the Bohemian crystal chandeliers, the hand-decorated doorknobs, the Hereke carpets and the walnut-and-rosewood furniture made by Abdül Hamit himself.

The 15th July Martyrs' Bridge stretching over the Bosphorus

5 15th July Martyrs' Bridge (15 Temmuz Şehitler Köprüsü)

C5

Built in 1973 to commemorate the 50th anniversary of the Republic of Turkey, this bridge was renamed in memory of the people who lost their lives here during the attempted military coup in 2016. At 1,560 m (5,120 ft) long, it is the world's sixth-longest suspension bridge. Pedestrians are not allowed onto the bridge, so if you want plenty of time to admire the view, cross at rush hour when the heavy traffic routinely becomes gridlocked.

6 Fortress of Europe (Rumeli Hisarı)

U2 ⌂ Yahya Kemal Cad ☏ (0212) 263 53 05 ⌚ 9am–6pm Tue–Sun

In 1452, as he prepared for his final attack on Constantinople, Mehmet II built this vast fortress at the narrowest point of the Bosphorus, opposite the Fortress of Asia (Anadolu Hisarı, *p98*),

to cut the flow of supplies reaching the city. The castle's three main towers are surrounded by a huge curtain wall with 13 bastions. The main tower later became a prison. Note that some parts of the fortress are being restored and might be closed to visitors.

7 Aşiyan Museum (Aşiyan Müzesi)

U2 ⌂ Aşiyan Yohuşu, Bebek ☏ (0212) 263 69 86 ⌚ 9am–5pm Tue–Sun

Famed poet and utopian philosopher Tevfik Fikret (1867–1915), founder of the Edebiyat-i Cedid (New Literature) movement, built this wooden mansion, now on the campus of Boğaziçi University, in 1906. It recalls the movement with the personal belongings and photos of the members.

8 Sakıp Sabancı Museum (Sakıp Sabancı Müzesi)

U2 ⌂ Sakıp Sabancı Cad 42, Emirgan ☏ (0212) 277 22 00 ⌚ 10am–6pm Tue–Sun 🌐 sakipsabanci muzesi.org

The summer residence of the Sabancı family of industrialists from 1951 to 1999, the Atlı Köşk (Horse Mansion) is now a museum set in stunning gardens that overlook the Bosphorus. The exhibits here include calligraphy of the Ottoman era and paintings by leading 19th- and 20th-century Turkish artists. The modern extension is an art gallery housing major touring exhibitions.

Exhibit at Sadberk
Hanım Museum

9 Sadberk Hanım Museum (Sadberk Hanım Müzesi)

◉ U1 ⌂ Piyasa Cad 25, Büyükdere
◷ 10am–5pm Thu–Tue ⬡ sadberk
hanimmuzesi.org.tr ↗

The Sadberk Hanım Museum features a must-see collection that includes a range of Turkish embroidery as well as Anatolian figurines, Assyrian cuneiform trade tablets, Hittite coins and gold jewellery.

10 Yıldız Palace (Yıldız Sarayı)

◉ C5 ⌂ Yıldız Cad, Beşiktaş ◷ 9am–5:30pm Thu–Tue ⬡ millisaraylar.gov.tr ↗

Though the core of this complex – the State Apartments (Büyük Mabeyn) – dates to the reign of Sultan Selim III (r 1789–1807), much of this rambling palace was commissioned by Sultan Abdül Hamit II. The park and its pavilions are also open to the public. Of note is the Great Mabeyn Pavilion and the panoramic Cihannüma kiosk. In the grounds is the Imperial Porcelain Factory, now mass-producing china where once they made fine porcelain.

Fortress of Europe, on the shores of the Bosphorus

A WALK THROUGH KARAKÖY

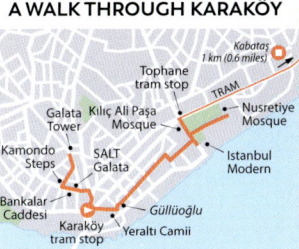

Morning

Start your day at the **Karaköy tram stop**, then head uphill to the early 20th-century Minerva Han, adorned with cupid statues. Turn left along **Bankalar Caddesi**, formerly Voyvoda Caddesi after Vlad the Impaler, whose decapitated head (it is said) was displayed here. If you have time, explore the **SALT Galata** art gallery (p60).

The **Kamondo Steps** lead towards the **Galata Tower**. Walk back along Karaköy Caddesi and turn right to visit **Yeraltı Camii** at Kemkaneş Cad 23, an underground mosque built on the site of an old Byzantine tower.

Afternoon

Continue along Karaköy and turn left onto Rıhtım Caddesi. The **Güllüoğlu** baklava shop here is the finest in Turkey; the Galata Rıhtım Köftecisi nearby offers a healthier option for lunch. Meclis-ı Mebusan Caddesi is home to two small mosques: the **Nusretiye Mosque** and the **Kılıç Ali Paşa Mosque**. Turn right onto the main road and, just after the Mimar Sinan University, turn right again. Follow the signs through the old docks to **Istanbul Modern** (p95), where you can watch the sunset with a cocktail in the chic café-bar overlooking the Bosphorus. Then take the **tram** from **Tophane** to Kabataş and the funicular up the hill to Taksim Square (p89) for an evening meal.

Lovely view from the Fortress of Asia

The Best of the Rest

1. National Palaces Painting Museum (Milli Saraylar Resim Müzesi)

📍 H1 📌 Dolmabahçe Cad, Beşiktaş
🕐 9am–5:30pm Tue–Sun 🌐 milli saraylar.gov.tr

Fine art dating from the 19th and 20th centuries is displayed in this museum, housed in the Crown Princes' Suite at Dolmabahçe Palace.

2. Çırağan Palace (Çırağan Sarayı)

📍 C5 📌 Çırağan Cad 32, Beşiktaş
🌐 hempinshi.com/en/ciragan-palace

Sultan Abdül Aziz spent a fortune on this confection of a palace, built in 1874, before pronouncing it damp and moving out. The Palace is now home to a luxury hotel.

3. Ortaköy

📍 C5

This pretty village beside the 15th July Martyrs' Bridge has many waterfront cafés, restaurants and clubs, and a weekend craft market.

4. Arnavutköy

📍 U3

Once noted for its strawberries, the village of Arnavutköy is now better known for the charming *yalıs* (wooden mansions) that line its waterfront.

5. Memory 15 July Museum (Hafıza 15 Temmuz Müzesi)

📍 C5 📌 Nevnihal Sok 12, Kuzguncuk
📞 (0216) 553 15 07 🕐 9am–6pm Tue–Sun

A modern museum commemorating Turkey's foiled military coup in 2016.

6. Küçüksu Palace (Küçüksu Kasrı)

📍 U3 📌 Küçükhsu Cad, Beyhoz (Asian side) 📞 (0216) 332 33 03 🕐 For tours: 9am–5:30pm Tue–Sun

Built as a lodge in 1857 for Abdül Mecit, Küçüksu Palace was a playground for the imperial court. It had two rivers known to the Ottomans as the "Sweet Waters of Asia".

7. Fortress of Asia (Anadolu Hisarı)

📍 U2

Built by Beyazıt I in 1391, this fortress on the Asian side is a smaller counterpart to the Fortress of Europe *(p96)*, added by Mehmet II in 1452, directly across the Bosphorus.

8. Emirgan Grove (Emirgan Parkı)

📍 U2 📌 Emirgan Sahil Yolu 🕐 7am–10pm daily

This park is a venue for the Tulip Festival *(p62)* each April.

9. Borusan Contemporary

📍 U2 📌 Perili Köşk Baltalımanı Hısar Cad 5, Rumelihisarı 🕐 10am–7pm Sat & Sun 🌐 borusancontemporary. com

A fashionable office block during the working week, Istanbul's coolest gallery at weekends, with great views of the Bosphorus from the roof terrace.

10. Anadolu Kavağı

📍 V1 📌 Asian side

This is the last stop for the Bosphorus ferry. Climb the hill to Yoros Castle, a ruined 14th-century Genoese fortress.

Bars, Cafés and Restaurants

1. Kaşıbeyaz
🔲 U2 🏠 Köybaşı Cad 10, Yeniköy
🌐 hasibeyaz.com.tr · ₺₺
This upscale kebab restaurant offers great views of the Bosphorus, good food and great service.

2. Feriye Lokantası
🔲 C5 🏠 Çırağan Cad 44, Ortaköy
🌐 feriye.com · ₺₺
Fashionable Feriye combines traditional Ottoman recipes with European flair. Booking ahead is advisable.

3. Kıyı
🔲 U2 🏠 Haydar Aliyev Cad 186/A, Tarabya 🌐 hiyi.com.tr · ₺₺
A smart and stylish fish joint in the posh suburb of Tarabya. The *meze* and fish mains are cooked to perfection.

4. Tuğra
🔲 C5 🏠 Çırağan Cad 32, Beşiktaş
🌐 tugrarestaurant.com.tr · ₺₺₺
Part of the luxurious Çırağan Palace Kempinski hotel, Tuğra serves superb Ottoman-influenced dinners in a fairy-tale setting.

5. The House Café
🔲 C4 🏠 Salhane Sok 1, Ortaköy
🌐 thehousecafe.com · ₺₺
The Ortaköy branch of this popular café chain serves unusual pizzas (such as pear, Roquefort and honey) and brunch staples. Its waterfront deck

is a draw during the summer months. Note that it is open for brunch only.

6. Any Café & Bar
🔲 U3 🏠 Arnavutköy Cad 71, Arnavutköy
☎ (0212) 265 32 69 🗓 Mon · ₺₺₺
Accompany burgers or pizzas with cocktails at this popular bar-restaurant. Live music and DJ performances are often held on the weekends.

7. Però
🔲 U2 🏠 Köybaşı Caddesi, Daire Sok 5/A, Yeniköy ☎ (0212) 223 77 77 · ₺₺₺
Cocktails with a Bosphorus view are the big draw here. Dine on eggs Benedict and pancakes in the morning, and steaks and salmon at night.

8. Atiye Bebek
🔲 U3 🏠 Çevdet Paşa Cad 15/A, Bebek
☎ (530) 829 71 81 · ₺₺
This popular restaurant serves refined Turkish cuisine in an elegant setting.

9. Blackk
🔲 U3 🏠 Muallim Naci Cad 71, Kuruçeşme ☎ (0212) 236 72 78 · ₺₺
DJ-led pop, R&B and other musical styles keep patrons entertained at this nightclub set by the Bosphorus.

10. Suna'nın Yeri
🔲 U3 🏠 İskele Cad 2/A, Kandilli
☎ (0216) 308 45 12 · ₺₺
The seafood at this modest joint is a fraction of the price of most Bosphorus fish restaurants, and just as good.

Fine dining on traditional Turkish dishes at Tuğra

ASIAN ISTANBUL AND PRINCES' ISLANDS

Asian Istanbul is just a short ferry ride across the Bosphorus or one metro stop through the Bosphorus tunnel. This area comprises the suburbs of Üsküdar, home to a few Ottoman mosques and the Maiden's Tower, and Kadıköy, with its lively bars. Between the two suburbs are the soaring Çamlıca Tower and German-built Haydarpaşa Station. Reached by ferry from Kabataş, the Princes' Islands make an ideal place to swim, cycle or simply relax at a harbourfront restaurant.

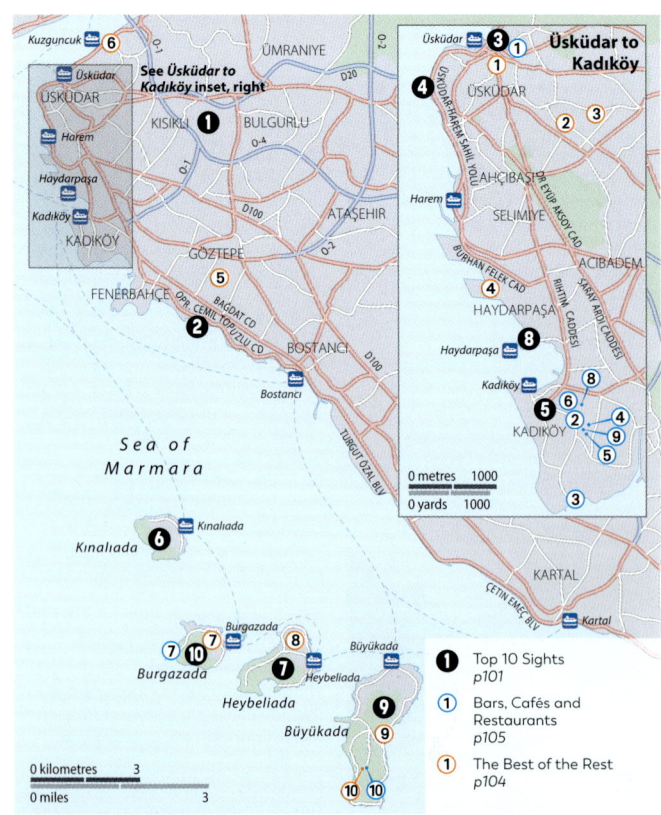

1 Top 10 Sights
p101

1 Bars, Cafés and Restaurants
p105

1 The Best of the Rest
p104

For places to stay in this area, see p117

1 Çamlıca Tower (Çamlıca Kulesi)

U3 Oyma Sok 1, Çilehane Yolu Cad 10am–10pm daily camlicakule.istanbul

Completed in 2016 and officially opened in 2021, this vast tower in Üsküdar is the tallest in Istanbul. Besides being used for TV and radio broadcasts, the futuristic tower also has a café, restaurant and two panoramic observation decks. Close by is the gigantic Çamlıca Mosque, which was completed around the same time as part of a major urban regeneration project.

2 Caddebostan Park

V5

This 20-km- (12-mile-) long waterfront park is one of the most pleasant spots in the city. Lounging in the grassy park is a favourite weekend pastime for locals – people enjoy leisurely picnics with music and books, and spend the entire afternoon here. A beach promenade with a bike path stretches the entire length of the park, ideal for e-biking, rollerblading or simply taking a scenic stroll. The park overlooks the Sea of Marmara, and the Princes' Islands in the distance. There are three beaches, too, offering activities such as windsurfing, beach volleyball and rowing.

Maiden's Tower, occupying an islet on the Bosphorus

Shrine inside the historic İskele Mosque

3 İskele Mosque (İskele Camii)

X2 Kurşunlu Medrese Sok (0216) 321 93 20 9am–6pm daily Prayer times

This beautiful mosque, officially the Mihrimah Sultan Mosque, was a present, built between 1547 and 1548, from Süleyman I to his favourite daughter, Mihrimah. Its raised portico offers fine views down to the main square.

4 Maiden's Tower (Kız Kulesi)

W3 (0216) 342 47 47 9am–9pm daily

This 18th-century tower is set on an islet in the middle of the Bosphorus and reached by ferry from a pier in front of the Ziraat Bank in Karaköy. It takes its name from a legendary Byzantine princess who was told that she would die of a snakebite and was locked up on the island for her own protection, only for a snake to arrive in a basket of figs. The tower famously featured in the 1999 James Bond film *The World Is Not Enough*. Today, it houses a small café and offers panoramic views over the water.

5 Kadıköy
📍 C6

Kadıköy, first settled as long ago as the Neolithic era, was the site of the Greek colony of Chalcedon, founded in 676 BCE, nine years before the establishment of Byzantium *(p8)*. However, Chalcedon proved to be more vulnerable to invaders than Byzantium, and it failed to flourish. Today, Kadıköy is a popular spot for shopping and clubbing, but it has still maintained its cosy, neighbourhood feel. The lively market area by the docks has stalls selling fresh fruit and vegetables and is a good, affordable place to buy provisions. A nostalgic tram rumbles through the area down to fashionable Moda, in Asian Istanbul, where you can enjoy a pleasant stroll along the seafront. Fenerbahçe – one of Turkey's top football clubs – has its grounds, Şükrü Saraçoğlu Stadium, close by, so expect traffic on match days.

6 Kınalıada
📍 U5

Translating to "Henna Island", Kınalıada is named for its reddish soil – a result of iron and copper mining in the past. The nearest island to the city and yet the least visited, it has some decent beaches and is popular in summer with Istanbul's dwindling Armenian community, which has a pretty church just above the village.

7 Heybeliada
📍 V6

"Saddlebag Island" is so called as the island comprises two green hills, with a saddle between them. The third island in the chain, it's an ideal place to hire a bike and cycle around. The Greek Orthodox Haghia Triada seminary *(p104)* dominates one hilltop. There are several beaches dotted around the island, but many have an admission charge.

8 Haydarpaşa Station
📍 C6 🏠 Haydarpaşa İstasyon Cad 📞 (0216) 336 04 75

Haydarpaşa Station is the largest station in Turkey and the most westerly train stop in Asia. Completed in 1908 by German architects Otto Ritter and Helmuth Cuno, it was a gift from the German government of Kaiser

Beautiful arches inside the Haydarpaşa Station

**Antique shops and hotels
lining a street in Kadıköy**

LINKING EUROPE AND ASIA

The first bridge across the Bosphorus strait was built by the Persian Darius in 513 BCE. After almost 2,500 years this was surpassed with the opening of the first Bosphorus suspension bridge in 1973. A second followed higher up the strait in 1988. In 2013, the Marmaray tunnel, running from Halkali on the European side to Gebze on the Asian side, was built. A third Bosphorus bridge was completed in 2016.

Wilhelm II. The Neo-Classical structure also happens to be on the site of a vast Byzantine tomb complex, discovered in 2018 during extensive restoration of the station. Over 50,000 Greek, Roman, Byzantine and Ottoman artifacts have been dug up, with more still being uncovered. Building work is ongoing, with the station due to become both Asian Istanbul's major rail terminus and a museum in the near future.

9 Büyükada
🚩 V6

"Big Island" is, unsurprisingly, the largest of the islands, and the furthest from Istanbul. Cycling is big here. Hire a bike and cycle to the Museum of the Princes' Islands (p104). Back in Büyükada, make the steep walk up to the Monastery of St George (p104) and the next-door restaurant – both with fine sea views of the Princes' Islands.

10 Burgazada
🚩 U6

The island of Burgazada is topped by a badly ruined Byzantine monastery. Of interest here is the museum of Turkish writer Sait Faik Abasıyanık (p104), which occupies a lovely period house. Visitors usually content themselves with a leisurely stroll, a splash in the sea or a fish meal along the waterfront.

A DAY IN ASIA

Morning

Take the tram to **Kabataş**. Make sure you have your Istanbulkart or buy a handful of single-use tickets at the ferry terminal. Pick up a timetable for ferry times. Summer weekends are very crowded, so arrive early to bag a seat on a ferry to **Kınalıada**. (The journey takes around 50 minutes). Visit the small **Armenian chapel** (*Akgünlük Sok Kınalıada*) on a hill just above Kınalıada's main settlement before catching another ferry south to **Burgazada**. Hire a bike and wheel around the coast to **Kalpazankaya** (p105) to enjoy a fine fish meal at the restaurant here. It overlooks a small beach where you can swim in season.

Afternoon

Ride the ferry onto **Heybeliada** and explore the harbour. Look out for the **Aya Nikola** (*İmralı Sok 11, Heybeliada*) Greek Orthodox Church and have a Turkish coffee on the seafront while waiting for a ferry onto **Büyükada**. To find out about the history of these islands, hire a bike and head for the **Museum of the Princes' Islands** (p104) on Büyükada's east coast. The best (albeit stony) beach is **Halik Köyü**, on the west coast. Alternatively, explore the town's *fin de siècle* mansions (Trotsky lived in one from 1929 to 1933), or walk up to the **Monastery of St George** (p104). The ferry back to **Kabataş** takes under two hours.

The Best of the Rest

Ornate interior of the Monastery of St George

1. Yeni Valide Mosque (Yeni Valide Camii)

⚐ X2 ⌂ Hakimiyeti Milliye Cad ⊙ Prayer times only

This imposing mosque was built in 1710 by Ahmet III for his mother, Gülnuş Emetullah.

2. Atik Valide Mosque (Atik Valide Camii)

⚐ Y3 ⌂ Çinili Cami Sok ⊙ Prayer times only

The huge complex of this mosque was completed in 1583 for Nurbanu Valide Sultan, the Venetian-born Jewish wife of Selim II.

3. Tiled Mosque (Çinili Camii)

⚐ C5 ⌂ Çinili Hamam Sok 1, Üsküdar ⊙ Prayer times only

Don't miss the İznik tiles, detailed with intricate floral and geometric motifs, inside this mosque, built in 1640.

4. British Crimean War Cemetery

⚐ C6 ⌂ Off Burhan Felek Cad

Most of the 6,000 Crimean War soldiers in this cemetery died of cholera rather than in battle. The War Memorial was erected in 1857.

5. Istanbul Toy Museum (Istanbul Oyuncak Müzesi)

⚐ U4 ⌂ Ömerpaşa Cad, Dr Zeki Zeren Sok 17, Göztepe ☎ (0216) 359 45 50/1 ⊙ 10am–6pm Tue–Fri, 10am–6:30pm Sat & Sun ⟳

Highlights of this collection of toys and miniatures from around the world include a French miniature violin from 1817 and a US doll from the 1820s.

6. Kuzguncuk

⚐ C5

Wander through the streets of this old Jewish quarter, then stop for refreshment in one of the many places to eat on the main street, İcadiye Caddesi.

7. Sait Faik Abasıyanık Museum (Sait Faik Abasıyanık Müzesi)

⚐ U6 ⌂ Çayır Sok 15, Burgazada ⊙ 10:30am–5pm Wed–Sun

Turkish writer Sait Faik Abasıyanık lived in this beautifully preserved home.

8. Haghia Triada Monastery (Aya Triada Manastırı)

⚐ V6 ⌂ Adalar Rum Kilisesi 45, Heybeliada ☎ (0216) 351 85 63 ⊙ 9am–12:30pm daily

The Turkish authorities controversially closed the seminary here in the 1970s. Today, it still functions as a monastery.

9. Museum of the Princes' Islands (Adalar Müzesi)

⚐ V6 ⌂ Aya Nikola Mevkii, Büyükada ⊙ Summer: 10:30am–6pm Tue–Sun; winter: 10am–5pm Tue–Sun ⊕ adalarmuzesi.com ⟳

The main draw at this museum is the many photographs that document the islands' modern history.

10. Monastery of St George (Aya Yorgi Manastırı)

⚐ V6 ⌂ Yuca Tepe, Büyükada ⊙ 9am–4pm daily

Set on a hill, this working Orthodox monastery dates to the 12th century.

Bars, Cafés and Restaurants

1. Kanaat Lokantası, Üsküdar

X2 **Selmanipak Cad 9** **kanaat lokantasi.com.tr** · **₺**

This traditional *lokanta* is as popular today as when it opened in 1933. It offers inexpensive and excellent Turkish food, as well as delicious puddings.

2. Polka Café, Kadıköy

U4 **Caferağa Mah, Zuhal Sok 19** · **₺**

A cosy little nook complete with red-and-white checkered tablecloths, Polka Café serves homemade cakes and excellent iced coffee.

3. Tarihi Moda İskelesi, Moda

U4 **At the far end of the pier, off Moda İskele Cad** · **₺₺**

In an ornate little building on the old quayside, this café-library serves coffee, tea and light snacks.

4. Kadife Sokak, Kadıköy

U4

Known to locals simply as Barlar Sokak ("Bar Street"), this lane is bursting with bars, cafés and clubs catering mainly to the young. Listen to avant-garde jazz or electronica in Karga (No. 16), have a beer on the rooftop at Stereogun (No. 10) or sit back and chill in Arka Oda (No. 18).

5. Buddha Rock Bar, Kadıköy

U4 **Caferağa Mah, Kadife Sok 14** **(0216) 345 87 98** · **₺**

This popular student bar has a wide range of cheap drinks, a delicious menu

of bar snacks, an energetic crowd and live rock and blues alternating with a DJ.

6. Çiya, Kadıköy

U4 **Caferağa Mah, Güneşlibahçe Sok 44** **ciya.com.tr** · **₺₺**

The kebabs in this gourmet restaurant are wonderful – the salads and *meze* are worth a look, too. If it's busy, visit the two other branches on the same block.

7. Kalpazankaya, Burgazada

U6 **Kalpazankaya Mevkii** **(0216) 381 11 11** · **₺₺**

A relaxed place on Burgazada's west shore with hot and cold *meze* and delicious grilled fish. Book ahead.

8. Deniz Yıldızı, Kadıköy

U4 **Serasker Cad 6** **(0216) 450 25 34** · **₺₺**

This long-standing *meyhane* in the Kadıköy *çarşı* (market) has live music on weekends and football screenings when Fenerbahçe is playing.

9. Viktor Levi, Kadıköy

U4 **Moda Cad, Damacı Sok 4, Kadıköy** **viktorlevimoda.com** · **₺₺**

Popular wine bar in the heart of Kadıköy, with a delightful garden. It has a range of decadent meals for lunch and dinner.

10. Yücetepe Kır Gazinosu, Büyükada

V6 **Kır Gazinosu, Aya Yorgi, Yüce Tepe** **yucetepe.com.tr** · **₺₺**

Next to the Monastery of St George on Yüce Tepe hill, this casual place serves excellent starters, savoury pastries, chips and grills.

Chefs preparing Turkish delicacies at Çiya in Kadıköy

STREETSMART

Lanterns for sale in the Grand Bazaar

GETTING AROUND

Whether exploring Istanbul by foot or making use of public transport, here is everything you need to know to navigate the city and its surrounding areas like a pro.

PUBLIC TRANSPORT COSTS

SINGLE JOURNEY

₺20

(zones 1–3)

TRANSFER FARE

₺14.32

(cost of second journey when transferring)

AIRPORT SHUTTLE

₺204

(from Istanbul Airport to Aksaray)

SPEED LIMIT

URBAN AREAS

50 km/h (30 mph)

INTER-URBAN ROADS

90 km/h (55 mph)

MOTORWAYS

120 km/h (75 mph)

Arriving by Air

Istanbul Airport is located on the European side of the city, 40 km (25 miles) northwest of the centre. **HAVAIST** runs private bus services to dozens of locations including Taksim (for Beyoğlu and Galata) and Aksaray Metro for (less conveniently) the Old City. The journey time is at least 45 minutes, depending on traffic. Istanbul Airport is also connected to the city centre by the M11 metro line. It takes around 30 minutes to travel between the airport to Gayrettepe on the M11.

The smaller **Sabiha Gökçen** airport is used mainly by budget carriers and domestic flights and is located on the Asian side of Istanbul, some 50 km (30 miles) from the city centre. **Havabüs** shuttle buses run to Taksim Square and Kadıköy half-hourly between 6:30am and 12:30am, taking a minimum of 1 hour. A taxi will cost around ₺1,000.

Havabüs
W havabus.com
HAVAIST
W hava.ist
Istanbul Airport
W istairport.com
Sabiha Gökçen
W sabihagokcen.aero

Arriving by Coach

Coaches arrive from several cities in Europe, including Berlin, Prague, Vienna and Sofia, with most services terminating at Esenler, 10 km (6 miles) northwest of the centre. Esenler is also the main terminus for domestic services, though some stop at Harem, on the Asian shore. Many companies offer courtesy buses from here into the centre; alternatively, ride the M1 metro.

Arriving by Rail

Istanbul is connected to the rest of Europe by rail. The best route from the UK to Istanbul is via either Bucharest or Belgrade and Sofia. Trains terminate at Halkalı, 25 km (15 miles) short of central Istanbul. Continue by Marmaray metro to the Sirkeci stop for the Old City. Get off at Yenikapı and transfer to the M2 metro for Beyoğlu/Karaköy.

Travelling by Metro and Tram
The most convenient and cheapest way to travel around the city is by metro and tram. Both systems are operated by **Metro İstanbul** and run between 6am and midnight.

The M1 line links the ferry terminal at Yenikapı with the coach station at Esenler, and the M2 line the Old City with Galata, Beyoğlu and Taksim. The Marmaray line runs west from Sirkeci to Kazlıçeşme, and east under the Bosphorus Strait to Üsküdar in Asia.

The tram route of most interest to visitors is the T1 between Bağcılar and Kabataş, which links the Old City with Galata and Beyoğlu. The T1 tram links in with the metro system at Karaköy (for the Tünel funicular) and Kabataş (for the funicular to Taksim Square and ferry terminal for the Princes' Islands).
Metro İstanbul
🅦 metro.istanbul

Travelling by Bus
Municipal buses are often crowded and get stuck in traffic. Sometimes, however, they are the only public transport available (running up the Bosphorus, for example), so you might have to use them.
Municipal buses
🅦 iett.istanbul

Travelling by Ferry
The main dock at Eminönü has departures to the Asian suburbs of Üsküdar and Kadıköy. It is also the departure point for cruises on the Bosphorus (p42). Ferries for Asia also depart from Karaköy , as do those running up the Golden Horn. Ferries to the Princes' Islands are operated by **City Lines** (Şehir Hatları) and depart from Beşiktaş, Kadıköy and Kabataş. Sea buses, operated by **Istanbul Sea Buses** (IDO), run from Istanbul Yenikapı across the Sea of Marmara to Bursa.
City Lines
🅦 sehirhatlari.istanbul
Istanbul Sea Buses
🅦 ido.com.tr

Tickets
To ride public transport in Istanbul purchase an **Istanbulkart**. You can buy a card and add credit at kiosks, stations and vending machines. To use it, simply touch the reader with your card as you enter the form of transport.
Istanbulkart
🅦 istanbulkart.istanbul

Travelling by Taxi
A licensed taxi *(taksi)* is yellow and shows a light on top when it is available for hire. Before you set off, always check that the meter is switched on. Better still, agree the fare with your driver before you get in. Beware of drivers taking the long way around in order to short-change you or those who wish to drop you off at the wrong location to avoid traffic. Some will not take short trips, as the journey time is often increased due to congestion.

Travelling by Dolmuş
Dolmuş (shared minibuses) are cheap, but can make for a slow journey. They run along set routes, but have no set schedule or stops. Instead, you can request stops by shouting "Inecek var" ("someone wants to get off"). Several routes start at Taksim Square; ranks have a blue sign with a black "D" on a white background. Note *dolmuş* will only depart when full.

Travelling on Foot
Walking is a great way to see the city, especially the historic core bounded by the Theodosian Walls. Unfortunately, streets are often unmarked, so it's easy to wander off track. Pavements may be rough and uneven, and kerbs high, so wear good shoes or boots. Traffic only stops at controlled crossings.

PRACTICAL INFORMATION

A little local know-how goes a long way in Istanbul. On these pages, you can find all the essential advice and information you will need to make the most of your trip to this city.

AT A GLANCE

CURRENCY
Turkish lira (TL)

AVERAGE DAILY SPEND

SAVE	SPEND	SPLURGE
₺1,750	₺4,250	₺7,500+

BOTTLED WATER	COFFEE	BEER	DINNER FOR TWO
₺20	₺115	₺150	₺1500

ESSENTIAL PHRASES

Hello	Merhaba
Goodbye	Hoşça kalın
Please	Lütfen
Thank you	Teşekkür ederim
Do you speak English?	İngilizce biliyor musunuz?
I don't understand...	Anlamıyorum

ELECTRICITY SUPPLY
Power sockets are type C and F, fitting two-round pins. Standard voltage is 220v.

Passports and Visas
For entry requirements, including visas, consult your nearest Turkish embassy or check the **Turkish Ministry of Foreign Affairs** website. To enter Turkey, you need a full passport valid for at least six months. Citizens of the UK, Ireland, the US and Canada can travel to Turkey visa-free for up to 90 days. Most people requiring a visa must apply in advance via the **e-Visa** portal. A multiple-entry tourist visa valid for up to 90 days in 180 days will be issued.
e-Visa
w evisa.gov.tr
Turkish Ministry of Foreign Affairs
w mfa.gov.tr

Government Advice
Now more than ever, it is important to consult both your and the Turkish government's advice before travelling. The UK Foreign, Commonwealth and Development Office (**FCDO**), the **US State Department**, the **Australian Department of Foreign Affairs and Trade** and the Turkish Ministry of Foreign Affairs offer the latest information on security, health and local regulations.
Australian Department of Foreign Affairs and Trade
w smartraveller.gov.au
UK FCDO
w gov.uk/foreign-travel-advice
US State Department
w travel.state.gov

Customs Information
You can find information on the laws relating to goods and currency taken in or out of Turkey on the **Ministry of Trade** website.
Ministry of Trade
w trade.gov.tr

Travel Insurance
We recommend taking out a comprehensive insurance policy covering theft, loss of belongings,

medical care, cancellations and delays, and read the small print carefully. Turkey does not have any reciprocal healthcare agreements with other countries so it's important to have comprehensive medical coverage, including repatriation by air. If buying a Europe-only policy, check it will also cover you on the Asian side of Istanbul.

Vaccinations

No vaccinations are required for Istanbul, but check with your doctor whether you'll need Hepatitis A or Hepatitis B vaccinations.

Money

Most places accept major credit and debit cards, such as Visa and MasterCard, and contactless cards. It's always worth carrying some cash around with you, though, for small purchases. Some attractions, tours and shops accept euros, US dollars and pound sterling, but any change will come in lira.

The many ATMs accept all Maestro and Cirrus bank cards with a PIN, and will also give a cash advance on credit cards. If you have cash to exchange, the best place to go is an exchange office (*döviz*). Most outlets accept credit cards.

Travellers with Specific Requirements

Istanbul still has some way to go when it comes to accessibility. There are few provisions for travellers who have visual or hearing impairments at even the biggest sights, and the city is quite difficult to navigate in a wheelchair owing to steep hills, high kerbs and cobbled roads. However, things are gradually improving. The tram and metro lines are wheelchair accessible. Many of the major sites such as the Ayasofya (Haghia Sophia) and Blue Mosque are partially accessible, and many hotels have one or more specially adapted rooms and wheelchair access to most floors. Specialist travel agencies, such as

Mobility Turkey, offer accessible package holidays and excursions.
Mobility Turkey
🅦 mobilityturkey.com

Language

The official language in Turkey is Turkish. Written Turkish uses the Western alphabet, but there are some differences in pronunciation (*p124*). In tourist areas, there will always be someone who speaks some English.

Opening Hours

Banks in main tourist areas open 9am to 5pm Monday to Friday, often closing at lunch for an hour; a few larger branches also open on Saturday mornings. Post offices open 8:30am to 5pm Monday to Friday. Shops are open from at least 10am to 6pm Monday to Saturday. Malls open 10am to 10pm.

Museum and sight opening times vary, though 9am–5pm is a useful guideline. The majority of the major museums and attractions such as Ayasofya (Haghia Sophia) and Topkapı Place are open by an hour or two longer between April and October than they are the rest of the year.

There are seven official one-day state holidays (*p63*): 1 January is New Year's Day; 23 April is National Sovereignty and Children's Day; 1 May is International Workers' Day; 19 May is Youth & Sports Day; 15 July is Democracy and National Unity Day; 30 August is Victory Day; and 29 October is Republic Day.

Istanbulites celebrate two principal religious festivals: Şeker Bayramı and Kurban Bayramı (*p63*). Many places shut down and daily life is disrupted.

Situations can change quickly and unexpectedly. Always check before visiting attractions and hospitality venues for up-to-date opening hours and booking requirements.

Personal Security

Violence against tourists is very rare in Istanbul However, the political security situation in Turkey is volatile, so keep an eye on the local news. Be prepared to undergo security checks and have your bag searched at the entrances to stations and shopping centres.

Visitors should avoid protests, which often take place around Taksim Square and by the Kadıköy ferry pier, as violent confrontations between riot police and demonstrators are not uncommon.

As in most cities, take precautions against petty crime. Report theft or other problems to the **Tourist Police**. Lone female travellers are occasionally subjected to verbal pestering and unwanted attention. Avoid walking alone in secluded areas after dark. If you feel threatened, head straight for the nearest police station.

Homosexuality is not illegal in Turkey, but it is frowned upon by Islam, and same-sex marriages, civil unions and domestic partnership benefits are not recognized here. Despite increasing levels of repression and official hostility, there is a thriving LGBTQ+ scene in Istanbul. Visitors can check out **SPoD** and **Lambda** for more details.

Lambda
🆆 lambdaistanbul.org
SPoD
🆆 spod.org.tr
Tourist Police
🆆 istanbul.pol.tr

Health

Turkey has a very good healthcare system and many people travel here for medical procedures. All visitors will need to pay for any treatment they receive, though, so comprehensive insurance is highly recommended.

Rabies is prevalent in Turkey, so be wary of Istanbul's many stray dogs and cats. Mosquitoes can be a problem in summer, so take some repellent. If you have a sensitive stomach, avoid salads and seafood from street stalls.

There are pharmacies (eczane) all across the city. Duty chemists (nobetçi), often stationed near hospitals, are open all night. Well-regarded hospitals include the **Amerikan Hastanesi** (American Hospital).

Amerikan Hastanesi
🆆 amerikanhastanesi.org

Smoking, Alcohol and Drugs

Smoking is prohibited in bars, restaurants, clubs and cafés, and there are no designated smoking areas inside. It is also forbidden to smoke on public transport.

The legal drinking age is 18 years. The legal blood alcohol limit for drivers is 0.5 per cent; those who exceed this will be fined and may lose their driving licence.

Penalties for the possession, use and trafficking of drugs are severe; large fines and custodial sentences can be imposed.

ID

It is a legal requirement to carry some form of ID at all times and pedestrians are stopped for random checks. There are also police checkpoints on many main roads. You should always co-operate with the officials conducting these checks.

Responsible Travel

Visitors can do their bit by walking around the city or using Istanbul's hybrid metrobuses instead of taxis, both of which help to reduce emissions. Wherever possible, also try shopping at places like Potlac Dukkan in Kadıköy, a volunteer-run shop selling crafts, clothes and jewellery hand made by local women.

Potlac Dukkan

W potlac.com.tr

Local Customs

Ninety-nine per cent of Turks are Muslim, but the degree to which they practise their religion varies. The country has become more conservative in recent years. Never make jokes about Islam, and couples should beware of displaying affection in public. When visiting mosques, shorts and bare shoulders are not acceptable; women may be asked to cover their heads with a scarf.

Do not joke about or criticize Turkey, its founding father, Atatürk, or the country's flag, as most Turks are very nationalistic and will take offence. Defacing a banknote (invariably adorned with an image of Atatürk) or the flag is a criminal offence.

Mobile Phones and Wi-Fi

Turkey's mobile phone system is compatible with UK phones, but US cell phones may not work. To save on charges, buy a local pay-as-you-go SIM or an international card from agencies such as **TravelSim**. The few remaining public phones accept credit cards or a phone card bought from a post office. Hotel phones are usually expensive.

The international dialling code for Turkey is +90. Istanbul has two area codes: 0212 for the European side and 0216 for the Asian side. To call abroad from Istanbul, dial 00 followed by the country code (61 for Australia, 1 for the United States and 44 for the UK).

Virtually all of Istánbul's hotels have free Wi-Fi, though some international chains do charge for the service. Many of the city's cafés have free Wi-Fi.

TravelSim

W travelsim.com

Post

Post offices and boxes can be recognized by a yellow and blue **PTT** (Post Telegraf Telefon) logo. Stamps can only be bought at post offices and PTT kiosks.

PTT

W ptt.gov.tr

Taxes and Refunds

Sales tax (KDV in Turkish) is included in fixed-price goods. Rates vary, but the most common is 20 per cent. Prices may rise if you ask for a KDV invoice – a trader who writes an invoice will have to pay tax. To reclaim tax on departure, shop at places displaying a tax-free sign and get a Global Refund Cheque to reclaim the tax (in cash) at the airport. You may be asked to produce the goods, so keep them with you.

PLACES TO STAY

Sultanahmet and surroundings are the heartland of Istanbul's tourist scene, with options ranging from cheap-and-cheerful hostels to boutique hotels in Ottoman-era townhouses. Across the Golden Horn, Galata and Beyoğlu are favoured by travellers interested in shopping and gallery-hopping. Here, you'll find apartments and period properties fronting the Bosphorus. Most places charge in euros. Prices tend to drop steeply out of season (November to early March, excluding Christmas and New Year).

PRICE CATEGORIES

For a standard double room per night (with breakfast if included), taxes and extra charges.

€ under €100
€€ €100–€350
€€€ over €350

Sultanahmet and the Old City

AJWA Sultanahmet

Q N5 **A** Piyer Loti Cad 30 **W** ajwa.com.tr/sultanahmet/mainpage.aspx · €€€

An extravaganza of Turkish opulence, this gorgeous five-star hotel features mother-of-pearl furniture, silk Tabriz carpets, original artworks, hand-painted ceilings and lashings of marble. The Afiya spa has its own mosaic-tiled hammam and an indoor pool. Enjoy breakfast at any time of day, a full pillow menu and free shuttle buses to the Old City – but note that it's an alcohol-free space.

Four Seasons Sultanahmet

Q G6 **A** Tevhifhane Soh 1 **W** fourseasons.com/istanbul · €€€

Within touching distance of the Ayasofya (Haghia Sophia), this honey-hued former Ottoman-era prison is an architectural beauty. Sunbathe in the landscaped courtyard, steam in the on-site hammam, satisfy your sweet tooth at the on-site patisserie and enjoy cocktails with a view at rooftop Sureyya Terrace.

Miniature Hotel

Q Q4 **A** Molla Fenari Soh 22 **W** hotelminiature istanbul.com · €

A three-minute walk from the Grand Bazaar, this 1875 townhouse previously served as a police station, a school and a newspaper office. Now, its ten serene rooms offer high ceilings, exposed brickwork and crisp white linens. It's worth having dinner at the on-site restaurant, if only to see its 140-year-old mosaic-tile floor.

Cheers Hostel

Q R4 **A** Sultan Cami Soh 15 **W** cheershostel.com · €

A stone's throw from the Ayasofya (Haghia Sophia), Cheers is something of an institution. There's a lively shared lounge and a mix of 6-, 8- and 10-bed dorms, plus en-suite double, triple, twin-bed and family rooms for more privacy. The staff organize BBQ parties every Friday and weekend pub crawls that start on the roof terrace.

Hotel Turkish House

Q G6 **A** Akbıyık Değirmeni Soh 40 **W** hotelturkish house.com/en · €

Just south of the Blue Mosque, this traditional Turkish house – built with 18th-century wood and oriel windows – has decorated its ten rooms with antique furniture and Ottoman wall motifs. It's worth upgrading to a suite for a bit more space. Look for the late-Byzantine ruins, preserved under a glass corridor.

Bazaar Quarter and Eminönü

Regie Ottoman

Q Q2 **A** Mimar Vedat Soh 5 **W** regieottoman.com · €€

Make sure you pay the bill at Regie Ottoman – it's named after the Regie Administration, an Ottoman-era armed tax-collection service. The mansion has 34 luxury rooms – opt for a deluxe with bathtub – and a romantic fine-dining restaurant, which had a star turn in the 2023 Michelin Guide; there's a small sauna and gym, too.

Mest Hotel

P2 Çiçek Pazarı Sok 22 mesthotel.com · €€

"Mest is Best", according to the guestbook at this sleek design hotel within touching distance of Yeni Camii mosque. It was built from 19th-century magnesite bricks brought here from all across Europe. These exposed brick walls form the backbone of the elevated room designs – some of which feature clawfoot baths, others mezzanine lofts.

Fer Hotel

P4 Türbedar Sok 12 ferhotel.com · €€

Fer means "brightness" in the old dialect of this area of Istanbul, and the design – which explores the reflection of light using high-gloss surfaces, mosaics and water – won this stylish hotel an award. The Fer attracts plenty of business travellers thanks to its sleek, somewhat masculine, rooms and fitness centre. Breakfast is a proper gourmet buffet affair, taken in the RoofFer Restaurant.

The Golden Horn, Fatih and Fener

Hotel Sultania

P4 Mehmet Murat Sok 4 hotelsultania.com · €€

Designed to make guests feel like members of the Ottoman royal family, the gloriously kitsch rooms at Sultania are named after famous sultans' wives. There's also a simple spa room offering massages, and a restaurant on the ground floor serving light bites and cocktails.

Orientbank Hotel

P2 Fındıkçı Remzi Sok 7 orientbankhotel.com · €€

An Autograph Collection hotel with the motto "East Meets Glitz", the razzamatazz of this place will either be a hit or a miss. It flaunts its All Butler Touch Service, where you can WhatsApp any request (restaurant reservations, tips for exploring) at any time of day or night. The hotel's Jazz Bar does a fine line in cocktails.

Beyoğlu

Georges

F2 Serdar-ı Ekrem Sok 24 georges.com · €€€

A glamourous French five-star, Georges feels both homely, thanks to in-house cat Lollipop and just 20 rooms and suites, and a treat, thanks to marble bathrooms and mahogany furniture. Perks such as in-room massages are also available. Le Fumoir, its French rooftop restaurant, has views of Princes' Islands.

Ecole St Pierre

F3 Galata Kulesi Sok 20 estphotel.com · €€

A short walk from the Galata Tower, this exquisite hotel is a renovated old French Catholic school built inside the grounds of an Italian monastery, with rooms that are a blend of modern and Parisian styles. Its courtyard boasts a rare remaining fragment of the original Galata city walls, built in the 13th century, and an upscale Italian restaurant. A real oasis of calm amid the city clatter.

Pera Palace

F2 Mesrutiyet Cad 52 perapalace.com/en · €€

The Art Nouveau Pera Palace isn't a hotel, it's an icon. Originally built to welcome guests arriving on the *Orient Express* from London, it was the first hotel in Ottoman Istanbul to have electricity – and an electric lift. Past guests include Zsa Zsa Gabor and Ernest Hemingway. Agatha Christie wrote *Murder on the Orient Express* in room 411, while room 101 is a museum in memory of Mustafa Kemal Atatürk, father of the Turkish Republic.

DeCamondo Galata

F3 **A** Felek Sok 2
W decamondo.com.tr/en/
decamondo-galata-a-
tribute-portfolio-hotel
· €€

There are two options at DeCamondo: Banque, on Bankalar Caddesi, and House, around the corner on Felek Sok. House is the pick, for its blend of vintage and modern décor, and its rooftop restaurant that specializes in tender charcoal-cooked meats.

World House Boutique Hotel

F2 **A** Galip Dede Cad 85
W worldhousebh.com
· €

This boutique hotel in a 130-year-old building punches well above its weight. High-design rooms feature exposed brick walls and wooden floors, plus there's an on-site coffee shop and a thin rooftop terrace with a front-row view of Galata Tower.

PeraNox Boutique Hotel

F2 **A** Tramvay Sok 5
W peranox-boutique-
hotel.hotel-istanbul.net
· €

A boutique hotel on a hostel budget, this extremely characterful home has a handful of standard and deluxe double rooms with exposed brick ceilings, white-panelled walls and small-but-smart white tiled en-suite shower rooms.

The Bank Hotel Istanbul

F3 **A** Bankalar Cad 5
W thebankhotelistanbul.
com/en · €€€

This sophisticated Neo-Renaissance-style hotel dates from 1867. The modern rooms, decked out in shades of brown and cream, are lovely enough, but it's the lobby bar or smart Serica restaurant, with its unique "soil to plate" menu, you'll want to linger in. There's also a spa and a bijou white-marble hammam.

Hostel Le Banc

F2 **A** Şah Değirmeni Sok 7 **W** hostellebanc.com · €

Sat above Café le Banc, which serves really good coffee, this sustainably minded bijou hostel has a 10-bed mixed dorm, a 4-bed family-only dorm and a private double, all in vibrant colours. No muss, no fuss and a great location.

Room Mate Emir

G1 **A** Sadri Alışık Sok 33
W room-matehotels.com/
en/emir · €€

Just a short stroll from the shopping paradise of İstiklal Caddesi, this intimate four-star design hotel offers real bang for your buck, thanks to the playful approach of Catalan interior designer Lázaro Rosa-Violán. Expect pops of pink in the glitzy lobby, mostly roomy rooms (those with a terrace are worth the extra money) and a sauna.

The Bosphorus

. . . .

The Peninsula Hotel

G3 **A** Kemankeş Cad 34
W peninsula.com/en/
istanbul/5-star-luxury-
hotel-bosphorus · €€€

Made from four buildings – three of them highly historic – this grand 177-room waterfront property is a spacious slice of serenity. There's a social-media-worthy outdoor swimming pool with stellar river views, a polished spa and wellness centre, and the top-notch Gallada rooftop restaurant with a Silk Road-inspired menu and distracting skyline views. Best of all, the hotel brought 650 new jobs to the area and achieved the top level of BREEAM certification for its sustainability.

Ciragan Palace Kempinski

U3 **A** Ciragan Cad 32
W hempinshi.com/en/
ciragan-palace · €€€

This luxury hotel is a former Ottoman imperial palace on the banks of the Bosphorus. An architectural marvel, it will have you swooning over the towering arched river gate and the use of mother-of-pearl inlay and imperial fabrics of blue and maroon in its sumptuous rooms and Neoclassical suites. Bring your snazziest swimming costume for photos in the infinity pool and a spot of pampering at the Sanitas Spa.

The Stay Bosphorus

U3 **Ortaköy Salhanesi Sok 1** **the stay.com.tr/the-stay bosphorus-hotel.aspx** · **€€**

This deliciously regal Ottoman family mansion is decked out in romantic velvets and billowy gauze curtains. To make the most of your liras, book the Deluxe Bosphorus Suite, whose balcony enjoys the same jaw-dropping views of Ortaköy Mosque and the Bosphorus Bridge as the Penthouse suites, but without the price tag.

Gezi Hotel Bosphorus

H1 **Mete Cad 34** **gezibosphorus.com** · **€€**

Almost a zero-emission property, thoughtful Gezi has earned Turkey's acclaimed Greening Hotel certification. It offers a range of minimalist rooms, the pick of which is the Loft, with its bedside Jacuzzi and views of Gezi Park. There's a spa, a bar and the Delma Grill Bar serving locally sourced Mediterranean fare.

VAKKO Hotel & Residence Sumahan

U3 **Kuleli Cad 43** **vakkohotel.com** · **€€€**

The owners of beloved Sumahan on Water sold their concept to fashion and lifestyle brand VAKKO – and this hip five-star is their baby. Splurge on one of the suites, which come with an in-room workout kit, wine rack, espresso machine and free-of-charge butler. There's also a gym, a stylish spa offering Ayurvedic treatments and a suave French restaurant.

Witt Istanbul Hotel

G2 **Defterdar Yhş 26** **wittistanbul.com** · **€€**

The 18 retro-modern loft-style rooms here are a design delight, with hardwood floors, Denizli linen sheets and marble bathrooms. The tasty breakfasts are organic, too. It's worth splurging on one of the lofts that has a panoramic terrace; if you can't, there's always the roof terrace with one heck of a view across the beautiful Bosphorus.

Asian Istanbul and Princes' Islands

Princes' Palace Resort

V6 **Çankaya Cad 58** **princespalace.com** · **€€€**

Break out the black AMEX for a stay at this serene hotel on the west coast of Büyükada island where Marxist revolutionary Leon Trotsky spent years in exile and wrote *A History of the Russian Revolution*. A world away from the bustle of the Old City, it sits on an estate with its own Beach Club (think infinity seawater pools and hammam), while the spa is billed as one of the city's best.

Splendid Palais Hotel

V6 **Yirmiüç Nisan Cad 39** **splendidhotel.net** · **€€**

Described by the *New York Times* as "an Art Nouveau-flavoured wedding cake of a hotel", this listed monument offers 60 opulent rooms and nine suites. It sits on the northern tip of car-free Büyükada island, looking out over the Asian side of the city.

Anastasia Meziki Otel

V6 **Malul Gazi Cad 24** **mezikiotel.com** · **€**

One of the oldest mansions on Büyükada, this family-run option has gorgeous antique-filled rooms with pops of pink, green and blue, plus an on-site restaurant with terrace. Look out for the console in the main hall of the first floor and the brass bed in the room to the right of the entrance; they belonged to the Karayan family who called this home until 1989.

Frezya Women Hotel

W2 **Eşrefsaat Sokağı 1** **frezyahotel.com** · **€**

Ideal for women nervous of travelling solo, this central women-only hotel offers modern rooms with added security measures for complete peace of mind. Rooms are clean, bright and equipped with a good working desk, fast Wi-Fi and a mini fridge.

INDEX

PHRASE BOOK

Pronunciation
Turkish uses a Roman alphabet of 29 letters: 8 vowels and 21 consonants. Letters that differ from the English alphabet are: c, pronounced "j" as in "jolly; ç, pronounced "ch" as in "church"; ğ, which lengthens the preceding vowel and is not pronounced; ı, pronounced "uh"; ö, pronounced "ur" (as in "further"); ş, pronounced "sh" as in "ship"; and ü, pronounced "ew" as in "few".

In an Emergency

Help!	İmdat!	eem-dat
Call a doctor!	Bir doktor çağrın!	beer dok-tor chah-ruhn
Call an ambulance!	Bir ambulans çağrın!	beer am-boo-lans chah-ruhn
Call the police!	Polis çağrın!	po-lees chah-ruhn
Fire!	Yangın!	yan-guhn
Where is the nearest telephone/hospital?	En yakın telefon/hastane nerede?	en ya-kuhn teh-leh-fon/has-ta-neh neh-reh-deh

Communication Essentials

Yes	Evet	eh-vet
No	Hayır	h-'eye'-uhr
Thank you	Teşekkür ederim	teh-shek-kewr eh-deh-reem
Please	Lütfen	lewt-fen
Excuse me	Affedersiniz	af-feh-der-see-neez
Hello	Merhaba	mer-ha-ba
Goodbye	Hoşça kalın	hosh-cha ka-luhn
Morning	Sabah	sa-bah
Afternoon	Öğleden sonra	ur-leh-den son-ra
Evening	Akşam	ak-sham
Yesterday	Dün	dewn
Today	Bugün	boo-gewn
Tomorrow	Yarın	ya-ruhn
Here	Burada	boo-ra-da
There	Şurada	shoo-ra-da
What?	Ne?	neh
When?	Ne zaman?	neh za-man
Where?	Nerede?	neh-reh-deh

Useful Phrases

Pleased to meet you	Memnun oldum	mem-noon ol-doom
Where is/are?	Nerede?	neh-reh-deh
How far is it to?	Ne kadar uzakta?	neh ka-dar oo-zak-ta
Do you speak English?	İngilizce biliyor musunuz?	een-gee-leez-jeh bee-lee-yor moo-soo-nooz
I don't understand	Anlamıyorum	an-la-muh-yo-room
Can you help me?	Bana yardım edebilir misiniz?	ba-na yar-duhm eh-deh-bee-leer mee-see-neez
I don't want	istemiyorum	ees-teh-mee-yo room

Useful Words

big	büyük	bew-yewk
small	küçük	kew-chewk
hot	sıcak	suh-jak
cold	soğuk	soh-ook
good/well	iyi	ee-yee
bad	kötü	kur-tew
open	acık	a-chuhk
closed	kapalı	ka-pa-luh
left	sol	sol

right	sağ	saa
near	yakın	ya-kuhn
far	uzak	oo-zak
up	yukarı	yoo-ka-ruh
down	aşağı	a-shah-uh
early	erken	er-ken
late	geç	gech
toilets	tuvaletler	too-va-let-ler

Shopping

How much is this?	Bu kaç lira?	boo kach lee-ra
I would like	İstiyorum	ees-tee-yo-room
Do you have?	Var mı?	var muh
Do you take credit cards?	Kredi kartı kabul ediyor musunuz?	kreh-dee kar-tuh ka-bool eh-dee-yor moo-soo-nooz
What time do you open/close?	Saat kaçta açılıyor/kapanıyor?	Sa-at kach-ta a-chuh-luh-yor/ka-pa-nuh-yor
this one	bunu	boo-noo
that one	şunu	shoo-noo
expensive	pahalı	pa-ha-luh
cheap	ucuz	oo-jooz
size (clothes)	beden	beh-den
size (shoes)	numara	noo-ma-ra
white	beyaz	bay-yaz
black	siyah	see-yah
red	kırmızı	kuhr-muh-zuh
yellow	sarı	sa-ruh
green	yeşil	yeh-sheel
blue	mavi	ma-vee
brown	kahverengi	kah-veh-rren-gee
shop	dükkan	dewk-kan
That's my last offer	Daha fazla eremem	da-ha faz-la veh-reh-mem

Types of Shop

antiques shop	antikacı	an-tee-ka-juh
bakery	fırın	fuh-ruhn
bank	banka	ban-ka
bookshop	kitapçı	kee-tap-chuh
cake shop	pastane	pas-ta-neh
chemist's/pharmacy	eczane	ej-za-neh
greengrocer's	manav	ma-nav
leather shop	derici	deh-ree-jee
market/bazaar	çarşı/pazar	char-shuh/pa-zar
newsstand	gazeteci	ga-zeh-teh-jee
post office	postane	pos-ta-neh
shoe shop	ayakkabıcı	eye-yak-ka-buh-juh
supermarket	süpermarket	sew-per-mar-ket
tailor	terzi	ter-zee
travel agency	seyahat acentesi	say-ya-hat a-jen-teh-see

Sightseeing

castle	hisar	hee-sar
church	kilise	kee-lee-seh
mosque	cami	ja-mee
museum	müze	mew-zeh
palace	saray	sar-eye
park	park	park
square	meydan	may-dan
information office	danışma bürosu	da-nuhsh-mah bew-ro-soo
Hammam (Turkish bath)	hamam	ha-mam

Transport

airport	havalimanı	ha-va-lee-ma-nuh
bus/coach	otobüs	o-to-bewss

bus stop	otobüs durağı	o-to-bewss doo-ra-uh
coach station	otogar	o-to-gar
mini bus	dolmuş	dol-moosh
fare	ücret	ewj-ret
ferry	vapur	va-poor
sea bus	deniz otobüsü	deh-neez o-to-bew-sew
station	istasyon	ees-tas-yon
taxi	taksi	tak-see
ticket	bilet	bee-let
ticket office	bilet gişesi	bee-let gee-sheh-see
timetable	tarife	ta-ree-feh

Staying in a Hotel

Do you have a vacant room?	Boş odanız var mı?	bosh o-da-nuhz var muh?
double room	iki kişilik bir oda	ee-kee kee-shee-leek beer o-da
twin room	çift yataklı bir oda	cheeft kee-shee-leek beer o-da
for one person	tek kişilik	tek kee-shee-leek
room with a bath	banyolu bir oda	ban-yo-loo beer o-da
shower	duş	doosh
porter	komi	ko-mee
key	anahtar	a-nah-tar
room service	oda servisi	o-da ser-vee-see
I have a reservation	Rezervas yonum var	reh-zer-vas-yo-noom var

Eating Out

I want to reserve a table	Bir masa ayırtmak istiyorum	beer ma-sa eye-uhrt-mak ees-tee-yo-room
The bill please	Hesap lütfen	heh-sap lewt-fen
I am a vegetarian	Et yemiyorum	et yeh-mee-yo-room
restaurant	lokanta	lo-kan-ta
waiter	garson	gar-son
menu	menü	men-oo
wine list	şarap listesi	sha-rap lees-teh-see
breakfast	kahvaltı	kah-val-tuh
lunch	öğle yemeği	ur-leh yeh-meh-ee
dinner	akşam yemeği	ak-sham yeh-meh-ee
starter	meze	meh-zeh
main course	ana yemek	a-na yeh-mek
dessert	tatlı	tat-luh
rare	az pişmiş	az peesh-meesh
well done	iyi pişmiş	ee-yee peesh-meesh
glass	bardak	bar-dak
bottle	şişe	shee-sheh
knife	bıçak	buh-chak
fork	çatal	cha-tal
spoon	kaşık	ka-shuhk

Menu Decoder

balık	ba-luhk	fish
bira	bee-ra	beer
bonfile	bon-fee-leh	fillet steak
buz	booz	ice
çay	ch-eye	tea
çorba	chor-ba	soup
dana eti	da-na eh-tee	veal
dondurma	don-door-ma	ice cream
ekmek	ek-mek	bread
et	et	meat
fırında	fuh-ruhn-da	roast
fıstık	fuhs-tuhk	pistachio nuts
gazoz	ga-zoz	fizzy drink
hurma	hoor-ma	dates
içki	eech-kee	alcohol
incir	een-jeer	figs
ızgara	uhz-ga-ra	charcoal-grilled
kahve	kah-veh	coffee

kara biber	ka-ra bee-ber	black pepper
karışık	ka-ruh-shuhk	mixed
kaymak	k-'eye'-mak	cream
kıyma	kuhy-ma	minced meat
köfte	kurf-teh	meatballs
kuzu eti	koo-zoo eh-tee	lamb
lokum	lo-koom	Turkish delight
maden suyu	ma-den soo-yoo	mineral water (fizzy)
meyve suyu	may-veh soo-yoo	fruit juice
midye	meed-yeh	mussels
patlıcan	pat-luh-jan	aubergine
peynir	pay-neer	cheese
pilav	pee-lav	rice
piliç	pee-leech	roast chicken
şarap	sha-rap	wine
şeker	sheh-ker	sugar
su	soo	water
süt	sewt	milk
tavuk	ta-vook	chicken
tereyağı	teh-reh-yah-uh	butter
tuz	tooz	salt
yoğurt	yoh-urt	yogurt
yumurta	yoo-moor-ta	egg
zeytinyağı	zay-teen-yah-uh	olive oil

Numbers

0	sıfır	suh-fuhr
1	bir	beer
2	iki	ee-kee
3	üç	ewch
4	dört	durt
5	beş	besh
6	altı	al-tuh
7	yedi	yeh-dee
8	sekiz	seh-keez
9	dokuz	doh-kooz
10	on	on
11	on bir	on beer
12	on iki	on ee-kee
13	on üç	on ewch
14	on dört	on durt
15	on beş	on besh
16	on altı	on al-tuh
17	on yedi	on yeh-dee
18	on sekiz	on seh-keez
19	on dokuz	on doh-kooz
20	yirmi	yeer-mee
21	yirmi bir	yeer-mee beer
30	otuz	o-tooz
40	kırk	kuhrk
50	elli	eh-lee
60	altmış	alt-muhsh
70	yetmiş	yet-meesh
80	seksen	sek-sen
90	doksan	dok-san
100	yüz	yewz
200	iki yüz	ee-kee yewz
1,000	bin	been
100,000	yüz bin	yewz been
1,000,000	bir milyon	beer meel-yon

Time

one minute	bir dakika	beer da-kee-ka
one hour	bir saat	beer sa-at
half an hour	yarım saat	ya-ruhm sa-at
day	gün	gewn
week	hafta	haf-ta
month	ay	eye
year	yıl	yuhl
Sunday	pazar	pa-zar
Monday	pazartesi	pa-zar-teh-see
Tuesday	salı	sa-luh
Wednesday	çarşamba	char-sham-ba
Thursday	perşembe	per-shem-beh
Friday	cuma	joo-ma
Saturday	cumartesi	joo-mar-teh-see

ACKNOWLEDGMENTS

This edition updated by

Contributors Jennifer Hattam, Emma Thomson

Senior Editors Keith Drew, Alison McGill

Senior Designers Laura O'Brien, Stuti Tiwari

Project Art Editor Tanvi Sahu

Editor Dharini Ganesh

Proofreader Elizabeth Dowsett

Indexer Helen Peters

Picture Research Team Virien Chopra, Manpreet Kaur, Samrajkumar S, Priya Singh

Publishing Assistant Simona Velikova

Jacket Designer Laura O'Brien

Jacket Picture Researcher Diana Jarvis

Project Cartographer Subhashree Bharati

Senior Cartographer James Macdonald

Cartography Manager Suresh Kumar

DTP Designer Rohit Rojal

Senior DTP Designer Tanveer Zaidi

Pre-production Manager Balwant Singh

Image Retouching-Production Manager Pankaj Sharma

Senior Production Controller Samantha Cross

Deputy Managing Editor Dharini Ganesh

Managing Editor Beverly Smart

Managing Art Editor Gemma Doyle

Senior Managing Art Editor Priyanka Thakur

Editorial Director Hollie Teague

Art Director Maxine Pedliham

Publishing Director Georgina Dee

DK would like to thank the following for their contribution to the previous editions: Phoebe Hunt, Melissa Shales, Terry Richardson, Helen Peters.

The publisher would like to thank the following for their kind permission to reproduce their photographs:

Key: a-above; b-below/bottom; c-center; f-far; l-left; r-right; t-top

First edition 2007

Published in Great Britain by Dorling
Kindersley Limited, DK, 20 Vauxhall Bridge Road,
London SW1V 2SA

The authorised representative in the EEA is
Dorling Kindersley Verlag GmbH. Arnulfstr.
124, 80636 Munich, Germany

Published in the United States by DK Publishing,
1745 Broadway, 20th Floor, New York, NY 10019, USA

A CIP catalog record for this book
is available from the British Library.

A catalog record for this book is available
from the Library of Congress.

ISSN: 1479-344X
ISBN: 978 0 2417 3514 5

Printed and bound in China

www.dk.com